Self-Esteem

Fast Proven Treatment For Recovery From Low Self-Esteem

Dr. Jennifer Alison

Table of Contents

Low Self-Esteem: The Curse We Must & Can Defeat

"We can change our lives. We can do, have, and be exactly what we wish."
Anthony Robbins

Living with low self-esteem can be extremely difficult. It can shape the way we think about ourselves and the people around us. It can be the force behind everything we do and don't do. It can be the deciding vote between happiness and unhappiness, success and failure. Having low self-esteem can make you feel hopeless. It can make you shy away from relationships and make it difficult for you to be assertive with the people in your life. Feeling bad about yourself can alter how you treat yourself and determine how you act around other people. You might find it hard to accept compliments and affection. You might allow yourself to be taken advantage of.

Most importantly, your self-esteem is unique to you. No two people with low self-esteem are exactly alike. We all come from different backgrounds. We all have different lives. This book does not assume that there is an all encompassing quick fix for anyone who struggles with feelings of low self-worth. Rather, it is designed to take all the things that make you unique into account. The journey it will lead you on should be personal and introspective. It should highlight the ways your negative self-beliefs have been shaped by your past and give you the skills to overcome them.

The methods in this book involve educating yourself about self-esteem and thinking back over your past to identify some ways in which your early experiences have affected the way you think about yourself. I will encourage you to make a variety of subtle changes in your daily life and give you the skills to let go of negative thinking and harmful habits. The road to healthy self-esteem may be longer for some than it is for others. It will require you to regularly reflect on your thoughts and feelings. You will learn how to better care for yourself, how to prioritize yourself and your needs, and how to be more patient with yourself.

A substantial part of this book will focus on the relationships you have with friends, lovers, and family members; emphasizing the importance of maintaining healthy boundaries. You will learn how to keep your relationships mutually beneficial and emotionally safe. By making gradual changes to your life and learning to listen to your thoughts and feelings, you will gain the self-respect and positive self-beliefs it takes to live the life you want. *Embarking on this journey takes bravery and commitment and you should be proud of yourself already for simply deciding that you want more out of life.*

"The only time you fail is when you fall down and stay down."
Stephen Richards

Part One: Self Esteem Without The Unhelpful Medical Jargon

In the first section of this book, I will cover some basic information about self-esteem and how it functions in our lives. I will encourage you to think about the ways in which your self-esteem affects you, including the effects it as on your home life, your career, and your relationships with others. I will discuss what it really means to have low self-esteem and how it feels. It can be extremely difficult for people with low self-esteem to accept praise and receive criticism. Therefore a large part of this section will discuss what feelings lay underneath these struggles and what you can do to make these parts of life easier. This section also covers the importance of treating yourself nicely in order to overcome your negative feelings about yourself. I will urge you to implement a regular self-care regimen into your life so that you can start building a stronger emotional foundation within yourself. Before moving on to part two, you will be encouraged to understand some common pitfalls and bad habits that could be contributing to your feelings of low self-worth.

If you are struggling with low self-esteem there are two things you should know right from the start. The first thing is that you are not alone. There are far more people in the world living with low self-esteem than you may think. It's important to remind yourself of that as you embark on your journey to positive self-esteem. Having low self-esteem can make you feel terribly alone in life and you might feel like no one understands what you're going through, but I promise you that is not the case. It's impossible to know what other people struggle with in their lives. Many people suffer from depression, loneliness, difficult relationships and low self-worth without anyone else ever noticing. For this reason I must start by stressing that, as you progress through this book and through life in general, comparing yourself to other people is a big 'no no'. Your self-esteem lies within you and that's where your focus needs to be in order to make positive changes in your life.

What is self-esteem?

Put simply, self-esteem is a way to measure your self-confidence based on how you value yourself in relation to other people and the world around you. Your self-esteem determines how important or unimportant you believe yourself to be. Because of its hold on your self-worth, self-esteem plays a key role in the relationships you have with other people, your working life, your mood, and your overall outlook on life. Self-esteem is a force within you that has the power to lift you up or pin you down. People suffering from low self-esteem often experience periods of low mood, depression, and anxiety. They may struggle with difficult relationships throughout their lives as well as shying away from taking risks in all avenues of life. People with low self-esteem are often more prone to self-sabotage via things like substance abuse, self ridicule and/or self harm.

"Wanting to be someone else is a waste of the person you are."
Marilyn Monroe

It is important to note from the start that your self-esteem is not set in stone. No matter what caused it to be the way it is - no matter what happened in your life that sent you flailing into the realms of low self worth - your self-esteem *is* changeable. You are the master of yourself and your life. You have the power to change how you feel about yourself. You have the power to rid yourself of negative self-beliefs and start to feel good about who you are. Be committed to yourself during this journey. It will not always be easy; embarking on a journey of self discovery and improvement is bound to be emotionally activating from time to time. Allow yourself to be brave and try to give yourself credit for your hard work along the way.

To begin, start thinking about what it looks like to have positive self-esteem? Take a moment to think about someone in your life who you perceive as having a healthy self-esteem. Ask yourself what it is about that person that makes you view them in this light. Is it something they have? Something they've achieved? Is it related to how they communicate with others or how they fit into the world around them? We hear the words *'good self-esteem'* a lot throughout our lives, starting in our school days and continuing through much of our adulthoods. But these words can be pretty ambiguous and elusive at times. It's possible that *'good self-esteem'* could mean something slightly different to everyone. For instance, you might think of someone else as having *'good self-esteem'* because you look up to them. Maybe you believe they've achieved more than you ever could. Or perhaps they have a beautiful home, a great job, a lot of friends, or an all around 'perfect life'. Maybe in fact, you feel the complete opposite way about the words 'good self-esteem'. You might think of someone with 'good self-esteem' in a negative light. You might be reminded of someone you don't get along with very well; someone who has bullied you or whom you've always thought of as arrogant, rude, or judgmental.

The truth is, having a good self-esteem does not make you arrogant or rude, nor does it mean being perfectly happy with absolutely everything in your life at all times. Having good self-esteem simply means that you believe in yourself and your capabilities. It means that you evaluate yourself and your achievements honestly and realistically. Most people with good self-esteem understand other peoples' feelings and are able to empathize with them. They don't feel threatened by other peoples' achievements, nor do they become devastated after receiving criticism. They don't beat themselves up every time they make mistakes or fail at something. Having a good self-esteem means having a solid sense of self, one that can withstand the inevitable ups and downs of life and not crumble beneath the opinions or judgments of others.

Having positive self-esteem *is* possible for everyone, no matter who you are or where you come from. It is not a measure of your achievements or success. Rather it is a measure of how you feel about yourself; something you have control over. It is never too late to change your views of yourself. Taking the time to get to know yourself, to understand your past and come to grips with your feelings, can dramatically change your self-beliefs. Once you've learned to evaluate yourself and your achievements fairly and realistically, you'll have the power to change your whole life and make it what you want it to be. By gaining respect for yourself, you will find that your relationships with others will become more satisfying, equal, and easier to maintain. The further you progress on your journey you will find your life goals becoming more easily attainable and your mood becoming lighter and brighter.

How does self-esteem affect you?

There are very few things in our lives that aren't affected by our self-esteem in one way or another. Almost everything we do is tied to our self-esteem in some way. Having a negative view of yourself can cause you to feel hopeless, paranoid, anxious, depressed, or lonely. It might mean that you judge yourself so harshly that you become inhibited and fearful in life. You might shy away from taking risks in your career, social life, or home life. If your sense of self is flimsy, you might find yourself being overly accommodating towards others. You might find yourself repeating relationship patterns that are hurtful or stifling or you might steer clear of relationships all together. You might find that you get taken advantage of regularly or that you are used and abused by the people you love. Having low self-esteem prevent you from being assertive, making it difficult to express yourself truthfully to your colleagues, friends, and family. As a result of this, you might find that people treat you as though you are inferior.

The list below summarizes some common characteristics of people with low self-esteem and looks briefly into the effects they might can on your life. As you read over these traits, think about how they might function in your life.

Characteristics and Effects of Low Self-Esteem

1.) Heightened Emotional Sensitivity

Many people suffering from low self-esteem are particularly emotionally sensitive. This can be immensely hard to cope with and one of the most difficult things to change about ourselves. Heightened emotional sensitivity can skew our self-beliefs in some very dramatic and detrimental ways. It can mean allowing yourself to be bullied at work or at home. You might experience regular bouts of mood swings and/or emotional outbursts. Furthermore, you might find it extremely challenging to accept criticism from others, feeling devastated by their judgments. If your emotional sensitivity consumes you, you might find it difficult to cope with stress and other negative emotions. You may find that experiencing rejection causes you intense anxiety, depression, and self-loathing. Recovering from conflict might be a real struggle.

2.) Negative Outlook on Life

If low self-esteem is causing you to have a negative outlook on life, it's possible that you'll experience regular bouts of hopelessness, pessimism, and listlessness. You might be reluctant to try new things or change the parts of your life that you don't like because of a deep rooted belief that things will never get better. These negative beliefs about your life can be very hard to overcome but if you don't challenge them, they will only hold you back from making your life what you want it to be. An overly negative outlook on life could cause you to feel jealous or resentful of others, and you might find yourself becoming bitter or cynical as time goes by. You may feel like 'giving up' constantly, often starting new things but rarely finishing them. You might be highly critical of others or the world in general. Having a negative outlook could lead you to neglect some of your own basic needs. You might not eat properly, get enough exercise or sleep, or spend enough time around other people. In more extreme cases you might become completely isolated or experience self-harming tendencies.

3.) Difficulties Socializing / Social Anxiety

Experiencing social anxiety is not uncommon for people with low self-esteem. Socializing is difficult when you're not feeling your best. It can feel like you are under a microscope or taking center stage with a spotlight shining on all the things you don't like about yourself. What's worse is that when you're socializing you might find that you compare yourself to other people and worry excessively about how others view you. In social situations, you might find it difficult to relax or calm yourself down. You might find it difficult to concentrate on conversations with others, feeling 'spaced out' or completely detached from the world around you.

People with social anxiety often struggle with memory loss, appetite disruption, and trouble sleeping. All of these things are common for people with social anxiety but the biggest problem is that life is, by nature, *social*. We cannot go through our lives without communicating with other people. Whether that means going out to a party, attending a meeting at work, or simply going shopping. Experiencing social anxiety can be one of the hardest things to overcome when your self-esteem is low, but I promise you, it's an obstacle that's worth beating. Overcoming difficulties like this will not only have a positive impact on your self-esteem, it could also present opportunities for personal growth, new relationships, and better opportunities in life.

4.) Self Doubt

Everyone experiences self-doubt from time to time but if you're struggling with low self-esteem, your periods of self-doubt could be excessive and debilitating. The more you doubt yourself and your capabilities, the harder it will become to believe in yourself at all. Eventually, you will find it hard to trust your own ideas, opinions, and even your own feelings. You will become more likely to refuse or negate compliments and praise from other people, thus potentially causing problems in your career and creating animosity in your close relationships. The more you doubt yourself, the more negativity you're directing toward yourself. You may as well be saying to yourself, *"I don't trust you and I don't believe in you"* on a never ending loop. You may become reluctant to prioritize your needs, to take risks, or try new things for fear of failure. You may become isolated and lonely. What's worse is that you might rely on other people for constant reassurance and approval. This can put unnecessary strain on relationships and cause people to pity or look down on you.

Self-doubt is a prime example of a belief system that does not serve you. All it does is add fuel to your self loathing fire.

5.) Feeling "Disconnected" or "Different"

Most people with low self-esteem have a tendency to feel slightly disconnected from the world around them or believe that they are entirely different from other people. The same can be said for people who suffer from depression and other mood disorders, as the feelings associated with mood disturbance are undeniably unique to the person experiencing them. However, the problem that can arise with this type of negative self-belief is that it places the self on the *outside* at all times. Believing that you are entirely different from every other human being on earth can very easily make you reluctant to join in with others. Whether that means socializing with friends and family, joining in at work, or developing intimate relationships. Furthermore, indulging in the belief that you are *different* can also give you the permission to treat yourself badly. It can be another way of telling yourself that there is something *wrong* with you, that you don't deserve the sense of belonging that other people feel.

When we stand on the outside looking in like this it's easy to view other people as though they are going through life with ease. You can imagine everyone else living a fairytale life with no problems or negative emotions at all. But this way of thinking is unrealistic and harmful. If you constantly view yourself as an outsider, joining in can seem impossible. If you constantly view others as positive, you will begin to view yourself as negative. Many people with low self-esteem experience tendencies to rebel or go against the social grain. They may have extremely low expectations of themselves and may struggle with substance abuse, eating disorders, financial troubles, and other unnecessary difficulties. The human experience is complex and it is different for every one of us. We are, each of us, *different* in many ways. In fact, *difference* is the one common thread that weaves itself through all of humanity. It's what we all have in common. For human beings, difference is what makes us the same.

6.) Fear of Intimacy / Difficulty Maintaining Close Relationships

Having low self-esteem can make it hard to develop and maintain close relationships. I will return to this topic many times throughout this book as relationships play a huge part in our lives. Whether it regards family, friends, colleagues, or sexual partners, a low self-esteem can be a relationship wrecking ball. Feeling unloved or unlovable can completely dominate your experiences where others are concerned. This could mean that you tend to have multiple short-lived relationships in rapid succession, that you avoid relationships entirely, or that you remain in dysfunctional or abusive relationships rather than ending them. If you are prone to self-doubt and mistrust, it can be hard to see the reality in your relationships. You might allow yourself to be taken advantage of or you might regularly take advantage of other people. You may be overly empathic towards others, suffer from excessive worry about how you affect them, or find it difficult to trust other people. People with low self-esteem often struggle to cope with conflict in relationships, thus causing them to feel anxiety, dismay, self-loathing, and even full blown depression over something as simple as a minor argument. Self-destruction and self-sabotage are common outcomes in these circumstances. Being assertive and expressing your own needs and desires can be difficult if your self-esteem doesn't allow for it. Navigating human relationships isn't always easy but by learning the right social skills, it is an obstacle that you can overcome.

7.) Excessive Nervousness / Panic Attacks

Nervousness and anxiety can be crippling for someone with low self-esteem. Panic attacks can arise at virtually any moment and they can send you into fits of nausea, tremors, and feelings of terror. Getting panic attacks under control isn't easy - it takes a lot of practice and determination - but doing so can completely change your life. Nervousness and panic can cause you to avoid pretty much anything. They can completely take over your life. If you've been experiencing panic attacks for a long time you might find that you no longer step out of your comfort zone. You might notice that your sleep is disturbed, that you dread daily tasks like going to work or shopping, or that you develop a number of new phobias in rapid succession. Furthermore, panic has a way of making us judge ourselves too harshly. It's common to become angry and frustrated about panic attacks but if you've got low self esteem, feeling unable to live a normal life can really hit you where it hurts. You may treat yourself unfairly, beating yourself up over all the things you struggle to cope with. It's important to recognize that nervousness and panic attacks are not your fault. They are *common* and *treatable*. These are

not feelings that you have simply made up and **they are not signs of weakness**. They are very real, human struggles that take time and patience to overcome.
Be kind to yourself where things like this are concerned.

8.) Perfectionism and Blaming Tendencies

It is important to recognize these two qualities as being indicative of low self esteem, despite the fact that people with low self-esteem are often painted as being weak and/or intensely under confident. The fact is, low self-esteem isn't always that obvious. Often, people with low self-esteem are the exact opposite of what you might expect. They might be known for their intense need to be the best at everything they do, being constantly active or busy, being bossy or regularly in positions of power, having issues with authority, and constantly seeking to appear as though everything in their life is perfect. All of these qualities are possible indications of people with low self-esteem. The need to overcompensate for ones' negative feelings about themselves can manifest in these positive-looking personality traits. It's almost a sort of ruse, a disguise. Certain people with low self-esteem are great at hiding it.

The problem with being a perfectionist is what happens when perfection is unattainable. If perfectionism is a mask for a flimsy sense of self, facing imperfection or failure can be extremely difficult. In a situation like this, a person with low self-esteem is more likely to blame others for what went wrong rather than being able to admit their own short comings. Blaming tendencies can also surface in a variety of other ways and they don't always involve other people. For instance, someone might blame the weather when they fail to get out for their morning exercise regardless of the fact that they have suitable attire. Whatever the case, when things go wrong the blame is always placed on external factors as the person with low self-esteem has an inability to cope with failure. The important thing to recognize with habits like these is the constant deflection of negativity; a reluctance to look inward at all.

"How would your life be different if... You stopped allowing other people to dilute or poison your day with their words or opinions?

Let today be the day...You stand strong in the truth of your beauty and journey through your day without attachment to the validation of others"
Steve Maraboli

Accepting Praise

It's important to note that having a low self-esteem doesn't usually stop at making someone feel a little under confident in life. Often, low self-esteem can hold you back from ever truly loving yourself or giving yourself the respect and fair treatment you deserve.

If you find it hard to accept compliments or praise from other people, how can you possibly praise yourself?

How can you recognize when you've done something worthy of praise if you constantly judge yourself unfairly?

Are you able to recognize when you've achieved something worthy of praise?

Do you allow yourself to enjoy your accomplishments (big or small)?

Would you say that you have a tendency to brush over the positive things you've done and focus instead on what you *haven't* achieved or what you wish you'd done better?

It can be almost impossible for a person with low self-esteem to treat themselves with the same kindness and generosity with which they treat others. In fact, many people with low self-esteem are extremely empathetic and warm toward other people yet they can be overly critical of themselves. They can easily see the triumph in other peoples' accomplishments and offer them genuine praise and celebration yet they struggle to do the same for themselves. They can fairly judge another persons' set backs and offer them kindness and support, yet it's a rare occasion that a person with low self-esteem will offer themselves the same courtesies.

People suffering from low self-esteem often shield themselves from positive attention, respect, and love. In life, everyone needs to feel lifted up from time to time. We need to be able to recognize the good in our actions and view ourselves in a positive light. This can be very hard for people who are used to putting themselves down or have difficulty seeing the good in themselves. For many people, offering yourself praise takes practice. If you know that this is something you aren't able to do for yourself - if you can't see the good in yourself, respect or love yourself - it's likely that you aren't allowing other people do it for you either. If you find that you're often batting compliments away like flies or avoiding situations where you might receive praise, attention, or recognition, you might be punishing yourself unnecessarily and starving yourself of the positive attention you deserve. This type of behavior can have an impact on most aspects of your life.

Ask yourself:

*How would you feel if your boss praised you in front of your colleagues? Would you accept the praise graciously or feel embarrassed and uncomfortable?
*Do you unfairly compare yourself with other people at work or within your family?
*Are you able to recognize your accomplishments and feel proud of them?
*Do you believe that you are inferior in work, at home, or in your relationships with others?

If you shy away from praise at work, you might reach a plateau in your career or get stuck in a job you don't like. If you think of yourself as inferior in comparison to a sibling or parent you might become resentful and withdrawn from your family. Learning to see the good in yourself and treat yourself kindly is a huge part of improving your self-esteem. This means being able to recognize when you've done something praiseworthy, giving yourself that praise and/or receiving praise from others, and being kind to yourself when you make mistakes.

Have a look at the following two exercises designed to help you get a grip on how you treat other people versus how you treat yourself. Remember that there are no wrong answers here. The primary aim of these exercises is to encourage you to start thinking more deeply about yourself and how self-esteem affects you.

Exercise #1

The aim of this exercise is to get you thinking about how you treat yourself in times of praise versus how you would treat your loved ones if they were in the same scenario.

Imagine a friend or loved one in a situation in which they have done something praiseworthy at work, school, or another public forum. Imagine them receiving praise from their boss, teacher, or a colleague.

Ask yourself the following questions:

How would you react to your friend receiving praise?
Would you feel uncomfortable? Jealous? Proud of them? Happy for them?
How would you feel if you congratulated them and they batted your compliments away or negated the sentiment?
How would you feel if your friend simply said 'thank you'? Would you think badly of them?

Now imagine the scenario *reversed.*

If you were the one receiving praise, how would you behave? Would you be able to simply say 'thank you' when another person congratulated you or would you counteract their sentiment with negativity?

If you are the type of person who finds it easy to praise other people but can't accept praise for yourself, take a moment to think about why this is.

From now on, when you receive praise or acknowledgement for a job well done, resist the urge to bat compliments away and challenge yourself to simply say 'thank you'. Doing this is a good way to start challenging the negativity to you feel toward yourself while training yourself to start thinking about yourself and your achievements in a positive light.

"To trust one's mind and to know that one is worthy of happiness is the essence of self-esteem."
Nathaniel Branden

Exercise #2

This exercise is similar to Exercise #1 but its aim is to get you thinking about how you would treat yourself in times of *disappointment* versus how you would treat your loved ones if they were in the same scenario.

Imagine you have just been criticized for a decision you made at work or at home. This decision is one you put a lot of thought into and one in which you believed you made the best decision you possibly could.

Ask yourself the following questions:

How would you feel if the people around you didn't agree with your decision and criticized you for it?
Would you be able to withstand their criticism and maintain your positive feelings about the decision? Or would your thoughts spiral into negative self-beliefs and catastrophic thinking as a result?
How might your mood be affected by a situation like this?
How might you behave?
How long would it take you to bounce back?

Take look at the following example:

Judy bought a new vacuum cleaner. She and her partner had often spoken about needing an upgrade and she'd gotten it on sale. When she brought it home excitedly, her partner criticized her for the purchase, insisting that she should've saved the money for an upcoming holiday they had planned. Judy felt hurt and embarrassed by the criticism and rather than being able to explain her decision assertively and have a reasonable conversation about it, her thoughts became focused on the negative. Even though she knew that she had plenty of money for the vacuum, her partner's criticism bothered her so much that she beat herself up for how stupid she'd been. She felt like she'd let her partner down and she couldn't do anything right.

In this example you can see how a relatively uneventful situation had the power to cause an onslaught of negative and catastrophic thoughts. This disagreement could've easily been solved if Judy had been able to assert herself and judge her decision realistically. But instead, Judy's negative thoughts consumed her. She experienced extreme feelings of worthlessness and even stupidity. If this self loathing could be caused by something as frivolous as a vacuum cleaner, imagine how Judy would feel if she'd made a more serious mistake. Imagine how badly she might treat herself.

Ask yourself:
How you would treat a friend in Judy's situation?
Would you tell them that they were stupid?
Would you ridicule them for letting their partner down?
Would you tell them that they're worthless because of a simple misunderstanding? Probably not.

Chances are, you would try to put the misunderstanding into perspective for your friend and offer them kindness and support. You would probably offer a few words of advice or encouragement.

When we speak to our friends in times of need, we're likely to offer them compassion and understanding but often the opposite is true when it comes to ourselves.

Think of an instance from your own past where you made a decision that was criticized by someone else. This can be something uneventful as the vacuum cleaner example or something with much more brevity such as quitting your job or moving far away. Think about how another person's reaction to your decision affected you.

Did someone else's disproval send your thoughts into negative or catastrophic territory?
If so, how did those thoughts inform your self-beliefs?
Did you punish yourself over it or treat yourself kindly in the face of adversity?
How long did it take you to recover?

Take a moment to identify how you treat your friends in situations like this. Do you treat yourself with the same compassion? If you tend to be kind to others but hard on yourself, take some time to think about why this is. The next time you face adversity, try to treat yourself like you would treat a friend.

One of the worse things about having low self-esteem is that you rarely know when to give yourself a break. It's as if there's a little voice in your head criticizing everything you do. It's constantly pointing out your mistakes. It tells you when you should've done better. It tells you when you should've said or done something differently. It tells you when you're acting awkward in public. It's the voice that replays all your embarrassing moments, failures, and rejections when you're feeling low. But that voice rarely tells you when you've done something right. It rarely gives you a pat on the back when you deserve one and it never consoles you when you need it to.

Learning how to silence that negative little voice takes time and practice. However, you can start by simply recognizing when your inner voice is being overly critical of you. When you hear your inner voice starting to put yourself down, practice treating yourself the way you'd treat a friend. Practice lifting yourself up after a fall. Practice being kind to yourself. Challenge those relentless negative self-beliefs that are constantly dragging you down. Treating yourself like a friend is a great way to practice judging yourself honestly and realistically. It will help you challenge yourself to let go of embarrassing moments once they've passed. And when your thoughts get trapped in that tornado of negative self-beliefs, you'll be able to challenge yourself to stop listening to them.

Remember, being overly critical of yourself will not help you do anything better. It will only restrict your courage and make you feel worse about yourself. Accept who and what you are. Accept that you will make mistakes from time to time. But know that defining yourself by your failures is an act of cruelty that you don't deserve. Leave the criticism to the rest of the world and free yourself from those overly critical chains.

"Remember, you have been criticizing yourself for years and it hasn't worked. Try approving of yourself and see what happens."
Louise L. Hay

How To Actually Practice Good Self Care

"You yourself, as much as anybody in the entire universe, deserve your love and affection."
Buddha

Living with low self-esteem often leads to harmful behavior; dangerous habits like being overly critical of yourself, beating yourself up over your mistakes, holding others in higher esteem than you hold yourself, and avoiding any risks that might lead to failure. Having low self-esteem is like being your own worst enemy. And if you're not on your side, who will be? If you don't approve of yourself or respect yourself, who will?

Believe it or not, if you want to overcome your low self-esteem, the one person whose love and care you truly need is yours. There are certain parts of us that will always be broken if we aren't hellbent on mending them. These are things about you that only you can change. You are the only person on earth who fully remembers your emotional past. You're the only one who knows what pain and memories have stayed with you throughout your life. Therefore, when it comes to recovering from your past and changing the things you don't like about your present, most of the work will have to come from you. *You are the master of yourself and your experience on earth.* If you aren't used to treating yourself with love and care, it's time to learn how.

Throughout this book, I will refer to 'self care' time and time again. But what exactly do those words mean? Put simply, self care means treating yourself kindly and engaging in activities for the sole purpose of your personal enjoyment and relaxation. These can be things like reading, playing sports, being creative, taking a long soak in the bath, or listening to music; anything that you can do that's just for you. Practicing good self-care is vital to your self esteem, your feelings of self-worth, and your overall physical and emotional health. Engaging in activities that are just for you is like bringing a friend flowers when they're sick, or surprising them with champagne in times of celebration. The problem is that most people don't spend enough time doing these things for themselves. We get caught up in our busy lives, rarely reserving any extra energy for ourselves. But if you're not practicing regular self-care, you're subconsciously putting yourself and your emotional wellbeing last on your list of priorities.

Your life may involve children who depend on you, a family member who needs special care, a partner, or a demanding career, but it's important to understand that if you don't take care of yourself, you won't have anything to offer anyone else. Furthermore, without spending any time or energy on yourself, you're sending yourself a very clear message, one that says "you don't matter". By implementing a routine of regular self care into your daily life, you'll be subtly telling yourself that you *do* matter, very much. You'll be actively feeding your soul. With a little practice, you'll get used to prioritizing yourself and your needs. It may be tough at the start but eventually self-care will become a part of your every day life. You won't have to think about it at all. And as time passes, you will start to notice the benefits. You'll feel better about yourself, you'll enjoy your life more, and these things will continue to get better all the time.

"There is overwhelming evidence that the higher the level of self-esteem, the more likely one will be to treat others with respect, kindness, and generosity."
Nathaniel Branden

If you struggle with periods of depression or anger, practicing good self-care is immensely important. It is equally beneficial to people who have trouble dealing with conflict or difficult relationships; be they romantic relationships, familial relationships, or friendships. A solid self-care plan can work wonders at both preventing periods of emotional disturbance and helping you cope with them. For most people it can seem impossible to engage in relaxing activities when times are particularly hard. For instance, if you're experiencing a moment of intense anger and you're struggling to calm down, you're unlikely to feel the benefit of baking a cake or giving yourself a facial! This is why having a daily self-care routine is so important. These activities might not be beneficial when you're having a particularly hard time, but engaging in them when things are easier can help prevent you from having such intense reactions to difficult situations.

People with low self-esteem are often quite sensitive and highly emotional. They may be quick to react defensively when faced with conflict or they may be completely devastated by it. If you find that you become emotionally activated quite easily or that you have trouble recovering from a period of agitation, self-care is extremely important for you. Taking the time to regularly treat yourself kindly can dramatically reduce negative reactions to emotionally challenging situations, while decreasing the time it normally takes you to calm down after such events.

There are endless amounts of ways you can implement self-care into your life - from hiking to painting to sports to exploring literature - but if you're not used to doing things like this regularly, you might find it difficult at the start. It can be hard to do something that's just for you when you're not accustomed to doing so. You might feel guilty about it or find yourself getting restless at the mere thought of it. But no matter how tough you find it at the start, it's important to stick with it. For instance, if you get in the bath and feel like getting out of it less than a minute later because there are other things you *should* be doing, resist that temptation and tell yourself to stay in the bath! Remind yourself that treating yourself nicely is also something you *should* do.

It's something you *have* to do in order learn how to prioritize your own needs and send positive messages to yourself. Paying attention to yourself and your needs and taking the time to treat yourself kindly is an *active* way to tell yourself that you matter. Being kind to yourself will help to contradict the negative ways you feel about yourself so that you can start building new, healthier self beliefs.

In the battle against low self-esteem, self-care is a powerful weapon. Remember, changing the way you feel about yourself is up to you. There is nothing anyone else can say or do that will make an impact as powerful as the one you can make. You hold all the cards. Make yourself a priority and dedicate yourself to this process. By learning how to treat yourself kindly on a regular basis you'll soon notice that you have a more positive outlook on life, more energy, and less anxiety in your day-to-day experiences. Your relationships with others will benefit too. Most of all, as time goes on, your self-esteem will naturally begin to improve.

Exercise #3

You don't need to wait until you've finished reading this book to start practicing good self-care! The sooner you start, the better. The purpose of this exercise is to get you into the habit of treating yourself kindly on a day-to-day basis.

Take fifteen minutes to write down 5 to 10 ways you can implement self care into your daily routine. These should be activities which you do solely for the purpose of personal enjoyment and relaxation. Be careful not to choose things that you can do while multitasking. Self-care is more important than grocery shopping and laundry! Furthermore, be sure that your choices are things you will actually enjoy. For instance, if you don't like taking baths, don't write 'take a bath' on your list! Think of things that you love to do but rarely make time for: meditation, reading, pampering yourself, taking nature walks, being social, baking, whatever floats your boat!

As the week progresses, aim to do at least one thing on your list every day. Don't worry if it feels strange in the beginning. If you're not used to caring for yourself in these ways or if you're the type of person who rarely relaxes, you might find carving time out for yourself a bit difficult. You may experience feelings of guilt or uneasiness.

However, in no time at all you will find that your new self-care routine becomes second nature. The best part is that while you're enjoying your 'me time', your self-esteem will naturally begin to improve. Think of these tasks as gently lifting yourself up, subtly improving your life and overcoming your poor self-image.

"To have an incredible increase in self esteem, all you have to do is start doing some little something. You don't have to do spectacularly

dramatic things for self esteem to start going off the scale. Just make a commitment to any easy discipline. Then another one and another one."
Jim Rohn

Dealing With Your Feelings In Good & Bad Times

In addition to practicing self-care, it's important to make time in your daily life to be quiet. In todays' busy world, most people get far less quiet time than they actually need. Nowadays we're in a constant state of stimulation and impatience. If we're not at work, we're surfing the Internet, watching TV shows, or getting sucked into the web of social networking. Even when we're in transit we're usually on the phone, reading, or listening to music. We are constantly being stimulated and rarely do we take the time to be alone with our thoughts. The problem with this is that our brains need time to rest and recuperate. If you are being constantly stimulated, how can you possibly make sense of everything that goes on in a day? When are you able to reflect on your life and your feelings?

Without enough quiet time in your life it's likely that your levels of anxiety will be constantly on the rise and your sleep patterns may suffer as well. Many of us purposely steer clear of quiet time completely because - either consciously or subconsciously - we're afraid of being alone with our thoughts and feelings. This is not uncommon. It's true that when you meditate or relax quietly with your thoughts, your mind might stray into unpleasant territory. Thoughts, feelings, or painful memories may cause you to feel negative emotions. Fearing these difficult emotions can make it challenging, even *frightening*, to immerse yourself in quiet.

The fact is, listening to your thoughts and feelings can be difficult and emotionally challenging, but doing so is a great way to get used to navigating difficult emotions. Everyone has negative feelings from time to time. We all have our own memories and life experiences that we find emotionally activating. **Unfortunately, ignoring or suppressing difficult emotions doesn't make them go away**. Although keeping yourself busy might help you ignore them for the time being, more often than not, suppressing emotions makes them come back with a vengeance. The longer you disallow yourself to feel difficult emotions, the more those feelings will fight for your attention. In order for you to get any relief from your pain, you must give yourself permission to be quiet and feel it. Allowing yourself to experience your grief, loss, sadness, anger, guilt, and loneliness might cause you some temporary emotional pain but this will ease with time. You will survive. Coping with difficult emotions isn't always easy, but you must remind yourself that your thoughts just want to be heard and your emotions just want to be felt.

If you're often restless, listless, or agitated, your brain is probably trying to tell you that you have some unfinished emotional business to attend to. This doesn't mean that you have to let your emotions overwhelm you or dwell on negativity; there is a fine line between feeling your pain and letting it consume you! Allowing yourself to experience memories and the negative emotions they come with doesn't mean allowing yourself become weighed down by them. By simply allowing your thoughts and feelings to flow into your consciousness rather than fighting them away, you will find that they flow out of it just as quickly. At times, being quiet might cause you to feel sadness, you might cry or feel frustrated in these moments, but there is almost always something to gain from them. You might come up with some practical solutions to your problems or you might simply notice that after your quiet time, your negative feelings have lost some of their sting. Living with emotions is a big part of being human and it's not always easy. But allowing yourself to listen to your feelings is vitally important if you ever want to come to grips with them.

Whether you take the time to formally meditate or just take some quiet time in the park, the car, or the bath, allow your thoughts and feelings to come to you naturally. Take notice of them and let yourself feel them. Then accept your pain and release it. Accept your feelings as true but temporary. Think of your emotions as being in constant motion, like clouds. Recognize their existence, let them move through you, then let them drift away. Your thoughts and feelings cannot hurt you; not in any sustainable way. Letting your emotions move through you means allowing them to be felt and then letting flow out of you. The more you practice doing this, the more you'll see your difficult emotions getting smaller and easier to cope with. And just like a blue sky, eventually those clouds will leave you for good.

Having a designated time and place to listen to your thoughts is a good way to get in touch with some of the negative feelings contributing to your poor self-beliefs. Remember not to dwell or beat yourself up. If you are prone to becoming low or depressed, set a time limit for your quiet time so as to prevent yourself from getting upset. Sit with your thoughts for fifteen to thirty minutes, then leave them behind you for the rest of the day. Remember, when you're uncovering things about your life that are particularly heavy or emotionally activating, go easy on yourself. Treat yourself gently and kindly. Show yourself extra love and care by doing things that you enjoy regularly. Take some pressure off yourself by getting plenty of fresh air, exercise, and relaxation.

"The best and most beautiful things in the world cannot be seen or even touched. They must be felt with the heart"
Helen Keller

It's important to remember that quiet time doesn't always have to be a negative experience! It can also be a great way to reflect on positive things that are happening in your life. People who are prone to bouts of depression or periods of low mood often find it hard to meditate on positive things. Their minds may lean toward the negative. If you have felt a lot of negative emotions in your life, they may have become your 'go to' emotions. Summoning up happiness, peace, and love can be difficult if you're used to feeling lonely, angry, paranoid, or depressed. If you find that sitting quietly evokes more negative emotions than positive, you're going to need determination and plenty of practice in order to gain control over your thoughts. You don't have to silence negative thoughts completely. Just allow them to come into your mind, recognize them, and then let them leave again. Try to bring your mind back to something positive after each negative thought arises. And when pleasant thoughts and feelings arise naturally, try to hold them in your mind for as long as your can. Focus on those positive feelings and let them feed and fill you.

Being alone with your thoughts is not always easy. Learning how to silence thoughts that are hurtful or negative is a skill that takes determination and persistence. When you're in a particularly fragile or sensitive state of mind, it can be hard to stop floods of negative or unhelpful thinking. During times like these, many people have a tendency to replay difficult experiences over and over in their minds. You may dwell on a recent embarrassing moment or find yourself indulging in reruns of conflicts or painful conversations. When you're finding it hard to love yourself, it can be easier to put yourself down than it is to raise yourself up. Living with low self-esteem may have caused you to have a tendency to kick yourself when you're down. You might dwell on things you regret or fret over things you're worried about. Try to remind yourself that regret and worry do not serve you; they are things that are rooted in the past and the future, things you cannot change. Meditate on life in the here and now.

Try using a mantra to keep your thoughts rooted in the present. Think: *Right here, right now, everything is fine*, or steady your breathing by thinking *let* with each inhale and *go* with each exhale. Alternatively try breathing through your nose without altering your breath at all. Just allow yourself to breathe normally and focus on the feeling of your breath as it touches your upper lip. Bring all your attention to that spot until your mind is quiet and you are settled in the present. Mindfulness and meditation take practice so don't fret if you have trouble keeping your thoughts from straying.

The important thing is that you continue to bring your mind back to the present and don't give up. If negative thoughts from your past arise, recognize them and let them go. Dwelling on these things will not serve you. If you have trouble carving out time for yourself at home, think about attending a guided meditation class. Keeping your mind in the positive present takes practice but it can do worlds for your mood and self esteem. It doesn't take long to feel the benefits. Indulging in regular quiet time can create an open minded, clear headed forum for you to find solutions to any problems you might be facing. It can help you think more deeply about your goals, you accomplishments, and the relationships in your life.

If you live with family or friends, tell them what you're doing so that you can make time for yourself every day without being interrupted.

This might mean waking up before everyone else and having a private meditation hour or a quiet cup of tea. If you find it too difficult to be alone at home, get some space at the beach, sit in your car in a parking lot and read, take a walk in the park, go to a cafe on your own and listen to the sounds around you, do whatever you can to send the right message to yourself. You are worthy of your own attention. You deserve time to yourself. You have the right to be free of negative self-beliefs.

"You have been criticizing yourself for years, and it hasn't worked. Try approving of yourself and see what happens."
Louise L. Hay

Putting a Stop to Bad Habits Forever

"Confront the dark parts of yourself, and work to banish them with illumination and forgiveness. Your willingness to wrestle with your demons will cause your angels to sing."
August Wilson

Thinking about patterns and habits that could be contributing to your self-esteem is an important step to take towards positive change. It's important to recognize what behaviors and thoughts of yours might need some tweaking. Everyone falls into patterns in life. We might take the same route to work every day or pack the same lunch day in and day out. These routines rarely cause us any harm, in fact our bodies and minds are designed to crave structure. However, most people have patterns in their life that are doing more harm than good and it is these patterns that we need to think about if we're going to make any substantial change in our lives.

Your thought patterns are likely to be directly related to your negative self-beliefs. Similarly, your behavioral patterns are likely to be at least partially responsible for holding you back from living the life you want. Whether they're stunting your career, your love life, or your overall happiness, any number of bad habits could be keeping you from really enjoying your life. Learning to love and respect yourself requires you to be honest with yourself. It's important to reflect on patterns and habits that could be contributing to your low self-esteem.

The following list suggests a number of bad habits that can have a negative effect on your life. As you read through them, be honest with yourself. Think about how these patterns might feature in your life. If you identify with any of them, think about when and why you adopted them and imagine what your life would be like without them. Once you've reached the end of the list, think about any other habits you have that could be keeping you from overcoming your negative self-beliefs.

1.) Focusing on Failure

When you're used to being hard on yourself, it's easy to get into the habit of putting yourself down. Individuals who have a tendency to focus on their failures rather than their accomplishments rarely feel good about themselves. Actively telling yourself that your achievements are worthless will directly affect how you feel about yourself. Think of yourself like a wooden post being hammered into the ground. Each time you unfairly criticize yourself for something you haven't done well enough, you're hammering yourself further and further into the ground. But there's only so much hammering a post can take, because as soon as you hammer a post too far into the ground, it becomes almost impossible to dislodge it. So too, the more you focus on failure, the harder it becomes to think of your accomplishments in a positive light.

In addition to beating yourself up over the things you haven't achieved, if you're used to focusing on failure, chances are you'll also have trouble recognizing when you've done something worthy of praise. Furthermore, you're likely to focus on things you could've or should've done better. It's not hard to see how this particular bad habit could eat away at your self-esteem. Think back to *Exercise #2* where you thought about how you would treat a friend in times of criticism versus how you would treat yourself. Remind yourself to be kind to yourself.

Breaking habits is hard work, especially if you've had them most of your life. Learning how to focus on the things you've achieved or done to the best of your ability takes practice. You need to learn to recognize when you're actively focusing on failure. Think about your behavior every day by reflecting on situations after they've occurred. Ask yourself if you really deserved the criticism you gave yourself or if you were wrongly downsizing your accomplishments. Identify if you were being too hard on yourself or if you were simply failing to see the positive in the situation. Once you're used to reflecting on your behavior like this, it's time to start implementing some positive self-talk. Instead of thinking about what you could've done better, turn it around and think about what you actually achieved. Resist 'buts' i.e. "I got a promotion but I didn't really deserve it" or "I got a lot of stuff done today but I should've done more".

And just as you did in *Exercise #2*, treat yourself like you would treat a friend. Would you constantly point out your friends' failures to them? Probably not. If you did they probably wouldn't be your friend for very long! Use your self-talk to lift yourself up, not to put yourself down. It's up to you to get used to doing this for yourself. Stop being your worst enemy and start being your best friend.

2.) Unrealistic Goal Setting

Goal setting can be a very positive force in life. Having your sights set on something you'd like to achieve can serve to motivate you and give you something to celebrate once you've achieved it. Goal setting can help us become our best selves. And there's nothing quite as satisfying as checking things off your to-do list! However, what happens when you're in the habit of setting unattainable goals for yourself? Chances are you'll be in a constant state of not-good-enough. Later on in this book, I will talk extensively about healthy goal setting but for now I'll keep it brief.

Setting your sights just that little bit too far out of reach can take away all the joy and motivation in the steps you hit along the way. Imagine wanting to change three things in your life. Let's say you want to quit smoking, lose weight, and increase your income. It's all you can think of for an entire weekend and suddenly there's no time to spare. Everything must go! You decide you'll need to lose at least twenty pounds by the end of the month. You'll quit smoking on Monday morning and start saving money right away. So you make some plans, maybe you write out a list or make a chart to follow your progress. Monday morning comes along and you're raring to go. You resist the temptation to have your morning cigarette, make yourself a green smoothie for breakfast, and go out to an early morning exercise class. Then you go to work but you're too distracted to get much done. Instead you think about what you'll do when you get home. You'll write a new CV, search the internet for a better job, write out a new household budget. You'll continue not smoking and have a simple green salad for dinner.

But soon you start to feel tired and quitting smoking is proving to be harder than you'd hoped. You persevere for another two days but then you'll decide that actually, you deserve a treat. Soon enough, the diet has been abandoned and the other two goals seem harder and harder to attain. If you're lucky you'll achieve one of your three original goals but chances are, trying to change too much too soon will backfire and you'll find yourself right back where you started, feeling like a failure. If you had set more realistic goals for yourself in a more realistic timeframe, you might've been able to achieve everything on your list. You would've ended up feeling proud and more confident. However, setting unrealistic goals has meant that nothing has been accomplished and your self-esteem has taken a big hit.

When you set goals for yourself, ask yourself if they're realistic. If a goal is unattainable, change it up. Give yourself more time or make the task itself more achievable. Think of goal setting as a tool to make you feel good about yourself, not a stick to beat yourself with when you don't accomplish what you set out to do.

3.) Self Sabotage

Self-sabotage is an interesting anomaly. It is yet another way you can be your own worst enemy and it can affect your life in a multitude of ways. Are you the type of person who often does something - consciously or unconsciously - to cause problems in your own life? For instance, do you often form relationships with people whom you know are bad for you? Do you allow yourself to enter relationships only to mess them up when they're just about to get good? This type of behavior is common in people with low self-esteem. It's as if there is a voice in your head telling you that you don't deserve love / affection / attention / success / happiness. And rather than silencing that voice, you listen to it and do something to destroy any chances you had at enjoying those positive experiences. Self-sabotage often makes people skip straight to the end of things rather than having to endure certain unpleasantries that may arise along the way.

For example, let's say there are some things at work that are bothering you. You feel like your coworkers don't respect you and your boss often overlooks your hard work. In a situation like this you have a few options. You can ignore the situation all together and remain unhappy at work, be assertive with your boss and coworkers and come to a resolution, or act out by coming in late every day and letting the quality of your work slip. Conflict and confrontation aren't fun for anyone so it's easy to see how daunting being assertive can be. However, you probably know that avoiding the situation will not be a lasting solution; eventually your discontentment will get the better of you. This is where self-sabotage comes in. If your feelings are stuck inside you and you're too scared to bring them up, eventually you might just crack. Maybe you'll tell yourself to just stop caring so much, develop a bad attitude. Maybe you'll decide to just go ahead and quit even though you don't have another job lined up or maybe you'll get yourself fired.

Behavior like this doesn't just affect people at work, it can also destroy relationships. You might find that your friendships rarely last or that your romantic relationships are constantly full of drama. You might have difficulties communicating with your family. It's important to note that self-sabotage usually arises when we are afraid of something; most often conflict or failure. If you're prone to self-sabotage, and you think you might fail at something, you're likely to abandon it all together or do something to make it impossible to achieve. Talk about being your own worst enemy!

Fear is a very real part of life and it's often closely linked to conflict and failure. The goal is to be comfortable enough in ourselves to be able to cope with these tricky parts of life. For instance, if you regularly end relationships because you're scared that you might mess up in the future, ask yourself why. What is holding you back from at least trying? Challenge yourself to revisit past relationships and ask yourself why you behaved the way you did. Similarly, if you struggle to maintain a job, ask yourself if self-sabotage is the true cause of that. It's important to learn to recognize when you're about to sabotage so that you can encourage yourself to express your feelings, be assertive, and face the conflict before it's too late. Dealing with conflict and confrontations may not be pleasant, but knowing how to navigate difficult situations is a skill that could change your life. Allowing yourself to face those fears rather than running away from them could increase your resilience when you're faced with adversity and make you feel better about yourself in the long run.

"Fear: False Evidence Appearing Real."
Author Unknown

4.) Focusing on Body Image

In today's world it's very hard to ignore the influence the media has on how we feel about the person looking back at us in the mirror. We live in times of perpetual fad diets, cosmetic surgery, and laser treatments designed to obliterate just about any blemish or unwanted strand of hair on our bodies. The people we see on television are beautiful and slender; no one looks their age, no one is an ounce overweight. Our magazines are selling 'beach bodies' in the summer and 'a new you every January. And if that isn't compelling enough, they make a point of highlighting every time a celebrity exhibits an extra half inch of 'flab' around their waist. In times like these, it takes a strong person to be able to ignore the how-to-be-beautiful onslaught we're subjected to. But as nice as it would be to be able to blame all of this on the media, often we're the ones pointing out our flab and wrinkles. We're the ones staring in the mirror sucking in our tummies and giving ourselves faux facelifts.

The thing about your body is that it is almost always a transient thing. None of us stay young forever, our weight will fluctuate from time to time, and sometimes we will have blemishes on our skin. The problem arises when we put too much emphasis on how we look. Seeking the perfect body is often a mask for something else we don't like about ourselves. Of course we should all strive to take care of ourselves. Concentrating on good health never hurt anybody! However, focusing too much on body image can make you hate yourself. How would you feel if a friend came up to you and poked and prodded your belly? How would you feel if they sat down across from you and said, *"You could really use some botox around your eyes."*?

If you regularly stand in the mirror frowning at your reflection, this is exactly what you're doing to yourself. Each time you criticize a body part, you're telling yourself that you're not good enough, you're not pretty enough, you're under par, you're overweight. No one needs anyone saying those things to them, so why are we saying them to ourselves?

The two most important things to think about when it comes to body image are: (1) body image can be used as a weapon against you and your self-esteem, and (2) if you're focusing on body image there's probably something deeper inside you that needs a little TLC. It's important for all of us to learn to love our bodies. We have to remind ourselves of the fact that the people on TV and in the magazines make up a tiny fraction of the human beings on earth. One of the most beautiful things about the human body is the fact that every single one comes in its own shape and size. We are all different, we are all unique, and that's a glorious thing! Think of your skin as your emotional armor. If you are constantly chipping away at it, eventually you'll penetrate your entire sense of self.

If you're in the habit of pointing out your physical flaws, it's time to stop. If you stare at your face in the mirror and imagine yourself with a different nose or a better smile, stop. If you poke and prod at your hips or dream about having different breasts, a different bottom, or someone else's body entirely, stop being so cruel to yourself! We are all born into our own skin and we have to learn to love it. Practice looking in the mirror and giving yourself a compliment every day. Resist the judgmental, perfect-body propaganda in the media. Seek to be in good health rather than driving yourself crazy trying to look like a celebrity. And when someone tells you that you look nice, don't negate their compliment. Just say, "thank you".

5.) Depriving Yourself of Joy and Pleasure

People with low self-esteem often have a tendency to deprive themselves of the nice things in life. This can come in the form of simply working too much and not taking enough time off, or it might be more of an automatic resistance to engaging in recreation. You might be the type of person who doesn't allow themselves dessert or nice vacations or you might find it hard to do nice things for yourself. You'd probably prefer to give gifts rather than receive them. This pattern relates strongly to the importance of practicing good self-care. We all deserve and *need* to treat ourselves kindly. But further to that, never allowing yourself the good things in life is an unnecessary restriction to force upon yourself. Tendencies like this usually tie in with feelings that neither you nor your accomplishments are ever good enough. People who struggle with this particular bad habit are often overachievers or people who might describe themselves as being 'hyperactive' or 'restless'. These people are so wrapped up in *doing* that they often forget about just *being*. They deprive themselves of rest and relaxation. They might work extremely hard at something but move quickly onto the next thing when it's finished, thus never allowing themselves to enjoy the product of their efforts.

If you have a tendency to be in a constant state of *doing*, it's important to ask yourself why this is. When someone is reluctant to sit down and/or rest, it's usually because they are avoiding something. This is almost always something deep down in their subconscious such as painful emotions or problems at work or within a relationship. It might be that this person feels guilty or regretful of something they wish they hadn't done or that they are struggling to get over a break up.

The problem is, avoiding your emotions by forcing yourself to be constantly busy can't last forever. Although at times being busy can be extremely beneficial, not letting yourself rest rarely is. It's important to maintain perspective if you have patterns like these. Whether you're working yourself to the bone or you're simply not allowing yourself to enjoy your favorite hobby, take a step back and ask yourself why. Are you avoiding thoughts or emotions that are difficult to navigate? By disallowing yourself pleasure, are you beating yourself up unnecessarily? Why do you feel you don't deserve a break? Is this belief rooted in something tangible or is merely a product of not loving yourself?

Keeping up with your self-care routine should help you combat these tendencies. Remind yourself that you deserve nice things just as much as anyone else. Your body and mind need rest and comfort in order to function properly. If you aren't allowing yourself the good things in life, it's time to start doing so.

6.) Neglecting Your Physical Needs

Taking care of your body is not just important for your physical health, it can also color the way you think about yourself and how you view yourself amongst others. In order to function properly, your body needs regular balanced meals, hydration, exercise, and regular sleep patterns. Neglecting any of these needs will have a direct impact on your health and your state of mind. Erratic mealtimes or sleep patterns can cause vitamin deficiencies, lethargy, headaches, weight gain or weight loss, chronic fatigue, attention deficit, and depression. Failing to eat balanced meals can have a world of ill effects on your body. Failing to get a substantial amount of exercise not only affects how you look and feel physically, but it also deprives you of endorphins, or 'feel good' chemicals, that are vital to your mood and energy levels. Not taking care of yourself is a form of self harm and it's important to think about what thoughts and feelings lie behind these behaviors.

If you're neglecting your body's needs, you're not doing yourself any favors. For one, your mind needs stimulation; getting fresh air and exercise is vital to its function. And furthermore, your body needs to know that you care about it! Taking care of your physical needs will directly impact how you feel about yourself. Your body deserves to be given its basic needs and your mind deserves to feel the benefits of them. If your life is lacking routine when it comes to your basic needs, start putting some rules in place for yourself. Get used to going to bed and waking up around the same time each night. Eat regular, balanced meals rather than reaching for unhealthy snacks throughout the day. *Be good to yourself.*

7.) Comparing Yourself to Other People

This is a dangerous pattern and we all have a tendency to fall victim to it from time to time. The phrase 'keeping up with the Joneses' comes to mind. Later in this book I will discuss at length how important it is to judge yourself by your own standards but for now it's suffice to say that comparing yourself to other people is dangerous! Whether we're in direct competition with people at work or we feel overshadowed by our siblings, comparing ourselves to other people is almost always a bad move. When we do this, we are forcing ourselves to focus on what we don't have; or more poignantly, our failures.

It can be hard not to envy other people's lives, especially when they seem to have everything. But focusing on other people is just another way of not focusing on yourself. We all have different lives. We come from our own backgrounds, we are the product of our own experiences. Comparing yourself to any other person is like comparing a banana to a tractor. It's irrelevant and pointless. Everyone feels 'different' from time to time, but it's the very fact that we're *different* that makes us all the same. Humanity is made special by the fact that we are all born into unique experiences, yet we are all still human. Our lives are equal. We mean as much to this world as our acquaintances do. It's important to remind yourself often that everyone struggles at times and no one knows what it's like to walk in anyone else's shoes. Your neighbors might look like they have the perfect family, but only they know what goes on behind their front door. Comparing yourself to other people is merely another way to focus on your shortcomings. It serves no purpose but to cause feelings of resentment and discontent. It can cause you to become depressed or cynical.

When evaluating your life, think about what *you* want out of it. Think about what you can change and what you can't. Think about how you can attain the things you desire and make plans to do so. Remember, you are worthy of having the life you want but it's up to you to make it happen.

8.) Substance Abuse

Drug and alcohol abuse can be detrimental to a person's self-esteem, self-worth, future prospects, and physical health. What's worse is that drugs and alcohol can be highly addictive and are therefore, often the hardest habits to break. Alcohol is a depressant. It can warp your perceptions of reality, affect your quality of sleep, cause erratic and/or dangerous behavior, and have seriously ill effects on your mood. Over time, the more you indulge, the more likely your health is to become compromised and you may find that you regularly experience extreme bouts of depression. Making a commitment to rebuilding your self-esteem isn't going to be easy and it requires a clear head. Reducing the amount you drink will benefit you great.

Furthermore, if you regularly turn to mind altering substances when coping with difficult emotions, it's important to think about the fact that a journey of self-discovery will be emotionally activating from time to time. Turning to drugs or alcohol could prevent you from being able to get perspective on difficult emotional situations. Using too much will likely slow your progress. In order to keep yourself emotionally safe, consider drinking less or stopping altogether. Stop all recreational drug use for the sake of both your physical and mental wellbeing. If you think you may have a problem with drink or drugs, seek help by reaching out to a friend, loved one, or healthcare professional. Make this a priority.

9.) Focusing on Things You Cannot Change

Most of us place our focus on the wrong things from time to time, especially when we're in periods of stress and emotions are running high. We focus on things that are we are completely powerless against such as the weather or our discontentment with hierarchies at work or school. We might focus on the traffic during rush hour or the frustration we experience when we're forced to wait in a long line at the grocery store. Habits like these are often second nature; that is to say, it's natural to feel negative emotions to some extent when faced with these daily occurrences. But allowing yourself to fall into patterns of extreme upset over them, or letting things like this overcome you is dangerous and pointless. Occurrences like these should not have the ability to shape your mood for the entire day. These are all situations and institutions we cannot change. It doesn't matter how upset you are about the fact that the traffic is going to cause you to be late. Your anxiety, anger, and frustration will not change anything about the situation at hand. They will only cause you extra stress, thus leaving you low on tolerance and drained of energy.

It can be hard not to become angry when things aren't going your way and it would be naive to suggest that it's possible to free yourself from negative emotions at all times. As human beings, we will all experience a spectrum of emotions throughout our lives. Anger, frustration, and anxiety are all 'normal' emotions. However, if you regularly focus on things you cannot change, it's important to start thinking about that habit more deeply.

What is it that you're avoiding by placing all of your energy on pointless endeavors and things you have no control over?
Are you focusing on the things you can't change because you're subconsciously avoiding the things you can? Is your misplaced focus a method of self-sabotage?
Is it a distraction from the things that are really bothering you?

Have a look at the following example:

Mark is unhappy at work and he'd like to get a new job. He's been feeling this way for a long time, a number of months or even years. Every week or two he searches for jobs online but nothing ever excites him. He decides to leave it for a while and lets a few more months pass, all the while becoming more frustrated with his current job and feeling low about it.

He's convinced that the reason he hasn't found a new job is either because
(1) there are simply just no good jobs available
(2) he'd need more qualifications to get the jobs he really wants
(3) he's found some jobs that he might like but he isn't sure if he'd actually get hired so he doesn't apply for any of them and tries to forget about them entirely.

Meanwhile, Mark only applies for one or two jobs the entire time, or maybe he doesn't apply for any. Can you see how all the focus here is placed on external things? In a situation like this, it's likely that something deeper is going on. Chances are, Mark is feeling under confident or scared of trying something new. He might be letting his fear of rejection get the better of him or he could be self-sabotaging by forcing himself to remain in a job he hates so much. Mark considers going back to school or volunteering somewhere but he keeps finding excuses not to.

Therefore, nothing in his life changes. He continues to work at his current job and continues to feel disgruntled by it. By focusing all of this attention on obstacles and things he has no control over, Mark is bound to ignore his true feelings and fears and continue being unhappy at work.

Here's another example of misplaced focus:

Let's say that Janet is unhappy with her body shape and she wants to get out and exercise more. She makes a plan to take a brisk walk every day. The first day goes great and so does the second, but on the third day, it's raining so she decides to stay in for the day. She tells herself that she'll get back to it the next day. But as it turns out, it's another rainy day so she stays in again. The following day she has to wait for a package to be delivered and she doesn't want to miss it so she spends the day in the house surfing the Internet.

The day after that she's in a bad mood. She decides that she needs new walking shoes so she may as well wait for the weekend to go and buy some. But the weekend comes and Janet is feeling a little under the weather. At the start of the following week she decides the kids need her at home. You can see where I'm going with this. By constantly focusing on the things around her, Janet is ignoring her own needs and desires. She's putting herself last on her list of priorities and chances are, soon she'll be beating herself up for giving up on her exercise plan.

Focusing on things you cannot change is usually a cover for something else. If you're in the habit of doing this, it's time to start thinking about what's really going on. Was Mark holding himself back from finding a new job because he was scared of failure? Was his low self esteem holding him back? Perhaps he was so anxiety ridden that he thought he'd be too nervous to attend an interview. Maybe he just knew deep down that he wouldn't be able to handle rejection if it came to that. Maybe his feelings about himself were so negative that deep down he didn't think he even deserved a better job.

Similarly, was Janet self-sabotaging because she was scared her new exercise regime wouldn't work out? Was it really the idea of failure that was keeping her indoors?
Was she focusing on all those external forces because subconsciously she didn't want to take responsibility for her own health and wellbeing?
Was she having trouble prioritizing herself above other things?

Perhaps she didn't believe that she deserved time to herself or maybe she was scared of being alone with her thoughts. One of the most important parts of self-exploration is taking time to reflect on why you do the things you do. What underlying thoughts and feelings are shaping your life? Ask yourself if you're focusing on external factors as a way to avoid more important issues.

Another point worth mentioning on this topic is the danger of focusing too much on other people. You might obsess about how another person thinks, how they act, or how they affect you. You might read into everything they say and do, making your own deductions about what their behavior means. Alternatively, you might find yourself constantly aggravated by other people a lot. You might focus on their short comings or behavior you don't understand. You might spend countless hours thinking about what other people should do, how they should change, how they could be better. You might think you have the answer to everyone else's problems and become frustrated when they don't listen to you.

Unfortunately ruminating about other people's lives is as unproductive as getting riled up over a traffic jam. Not only can it be a source of added frustration in your life, but it's also another way of starving yourself of the attention you deserve, ignoring things about yourself that you'd like to change. When you find yourself thinking about other people's lives, think about why you're doing it. Are you thinking about other people to avoid thinking about yourself? Is there something negative about another person that you identify with but are too scared to face?

Encourage yourself to explore your tendencies to focus on things you can't change and put a stop to it if and when you can. Reserve your energy for bettering yourself and your life.

10.) Focusing on Past Mistakes

"All changes, even the most longed for, have their melancholy; for what we leave behind us is a part of ourselves; we must die to one life before we can enter another."
Anatole France

It can be hard to let go of things that happened in the past. Whether they were traumatic events from your childhood or things you regret. If you have a hard time letting go of events from your past, it can feel like you're carrying them around with you wherever you go; baggage that weighs on your neck and shoulders. You may experience flashbacks of events you'd rather forget or you might feel forever changed by your past experiences.

Coping with events from the past can be one of the hardest parts of life. We may grieve people we've loved and lost for as long as we live. Many things will stay with us for our entire lives but some things are better left in the past. Thinking too much about past events that cause you feelings of guilt and regret can act as an emotional anchor. They can cause anxiety, fear of intimacy, self-loathing, longing, and depression, to name a few. If you're in a particularly fragile state, the mind can have a way of rerunning past experiences wherein you felt embarrassed or you behaved in a way you wish you hadn't.

These could be things that happened in your distant past, things that no one remembers but you. You might have said something stupid at a party ten years ago and find that every once in a while, it *still* echoes in your head. You might think often about times you were rejected by lovers, friends, or family members. These reruns from the past could literally span from something as simple as a time you mispronounced a word to a time you caused another person serious pain.

The problem here is very similar to that above: dwelling on the past is as pointless as focusing on things you can't change. Unfortunately, things from the past can be a lot more harmful. When we focus on our mistakes, our shortcomings, or our feelings of guilt, we're keeping ourselves rooted in painful emotions. You cannot change the past but it can still hurt you, especially when you're feeling low. Think of negative experiences from your past like seeds. When they originally occurred, they planted themselves deep within you and each time you've experienced a similar situation, those seeds have been watered. Even in the present these seeds continue to grow, get stronger, and may even haunt you.

It's easy to use your past mistakes to beat yourself up. It's easy to let these things dictate how you live in the here and now. For instance, if you've gone through a particularly difficult relationship, you might close yourself off to the idea of love entirely, choosing to live a life of solitude rather than trying again. Or if you made a stupid mistake at a party, you might develop social anxiety and choose to avoid social gatherings wherever possible. Letting go of the past can take a long time but if you think your past has a hold on your present, it's time to make a change. We may not be able to change the past, but we can recover from it. *Your past is not the ruler of you.*

Your mistakes do not define you. The fact that you once made a mistake does not mean that you're bound to repeat it. Forgive yourself for your mistakes. Leave your embarrassing moments behind you. Focus on who you are now. Focus on what you can do now. Think about what your future looks like without carrying all that excess baggage around with you.

You deserve to feel lighter. You deserve enjoyment in your life.

Exercise #4

Before moving on to Part Two, look back over the harmful habits listed above. Take some time to think about yourself and any things that might be getting in the way of your happiness. Make a note of any patterns that sound familiar to you in your life. This could include one habit or all of the above! When you are finished, write down any other bad habits you have that aren't listed here.

When you've finished, look over your list and make a resolve to put a stop to your harmful patterns. Put your list somewhere that you'll be able to see it every day. Take time each day to look at it and encourage yourself to break your bad habits.

Every time you resist falling into the hands of an old habit, remember to feel proud of your accomplishment. Changing habits is not an easy task so it's important that you give yourself credit every time you make progress. You are actively taking steps towards ditching your negative self-beliefs! Pat yourself on the back and reward yourself as you progress. You deserve to feel good about every step you take towards a happier future!

Part Two: Moving On, Building Confidence, Building Esteem

"Optimism is the faith that leads to achievement. Nothing can be done without hope and confidence."
Helen Keller

In Part One I talked a lot about how your self-esteem functions in your daily life. I discussed some common difficulties that people with low self-esteem face throughout their lives as well as some harmful habits that might be holding you back from loving yourself and truly enjoying your life. In addition I touched briefly on the topics of receiving praise and coping with disappointment. You learned that practicing good self-care and getting plenty of quiet time can lift your mood dramatically while preventing periods of depression and heightened emotional sensitivity. Doing these things on a regular basis can sustain periods of good mood. It can serve to make your periods of low mood strike less often and make them easier to cope with.

In Part Two you will learn about how your childhood experiences have affected your self-esteem and how they may have contributed to your negative self beliefs. I will talk extensively about your relationships with your parents and/or any other primary caregivers you may have had as a child. I will encourage you to explore the ways in which your early experiences informed how you perceived yourself and the world around you. This section also covers your fundamental human needs and how difficulties in your childhood may have prevented you from acquiring them. This in turn, will lead to discussions about how you may be lacking some of your fundamental needs in adulthood. Towards the end of this section I will talk about the importance of healthy boundaries in your relationships with friends, family, and coworkers. I will touch upon how being selfless can both help and harm you. Lastly, I will focus on the function of self-esteem in romantic relationships.

It is important to note that some of the topics in this section can be emotionally activating. You may be reminded of events from your past that were painful or difficult. You may feel apprehensive when revisiting things you haven't thought about in many years. Thinking about our early experiences and the relationships we had with our parents can bring up negative emotions so please remember to treat yourself kindly as you progress through this section.

Be sure to give yourself plenty of self-care and try to take this part of your journey slowly. Journeys of self-discovery take time and patience. If you find these topics particularly challenging, take a break for a while and return when you are feeling up to it. As always, if you find yourself feeling depressed or you think you are in danger of hurting yourself or any one else, do not proceed and please seek help immediately.

What causes self-esteem?

Low self-esteem isn't something you were just born with, nor is it something you have to live with for the rest of your days. It's important to understand how your self beliefs were originally formed in order to be able to challenge and overcome them. For some people just lightly retracing your steps is enough to lead you to some conclusions about where things went wrong and how you can fix them. For others, deeper exploration might be necessary. Remember, with knowledge comes power. Understanding the things that made us who we are is a powerful weapon against the difficulties we face in the here and now. The more you understand about yourself and your feelings, the more you'll be able to challenge your negative self beliefs and start building a more positive view of yourself.

You and your self-esteem are unique. Every single person on earth has their own physiological make up and their own experiences that have contributed to their self beliefs. There has never been another person on earth who's had the same life as you and there never will be. Even siblings who grew up in the same home can have dramatically different experiences from one another. They may have entirely different feelings about their childhoods and they may grow up to have vastly different lives. As you have progressed through life you've developed your own feelings, beliefs and values based on your own individual experiences in the world. These beliefs began being formed in the early days of your childhood. They continued to grow and change throughout your adolescence and eventually joined you in adulthood. Your school life, working life, and your relationships with friends and lovers all contribute to how you feel about yourself and the world around you. So too, all of your experiences of joy, love, sadness, and grief inform how you react to different situations as you grow older. Every facet of your life plays a part in who you are and how you feel about yourself.

If you take a minute or so to imagine some events in your life that may have played a part in shaping who you are, chances are quite a few things will pop into your mind. You might remember a certain person or place that had a significant effect on you. You might think back to an event that was particularly joyous or painful. You might be reminded of an unfulfilled aspiration you once had or a goal you never reached. You might even remember specific words that another person once said to you that you found helpful or harmful.

Because everyone's past is packed with thousands of individual experiences on a spectrum ranging from devastating to exalting, in a way we are all carrying our past experiences into every new experience we have. Each person's life experiences have informed - and continue to inform - their life choices, both good and bad. Their experiences have informed how they treat other people, how they allow other people to treat them, how brave or meek they are, how they react to criticism and praise, and virtually every other aspect of their lives. Most importantly, everyone's life experiences are responsible for shaping their self esteems: high, low, and everywhere in between.

The idea of revisiting painful events in your life that can stir up some feelings of apprehension. These feelings are completely natural. During a process of self exploration, it's common to feel emotionally activated from time to time. It's important to take your time during this process. Try not to push yourself too hard and to remember to give yourself regular breaks and plenty of praise. It takes courage to think back over times that were upsetting, not to mention how much dedication you'll be putting into changing how you feel about yourself. Be sure to implement some methods of self care into your daily life during this time and make sure to give yourself credit for your hard work every step along the way. Remember, you do not have to live with low self-esteem or negative self beliefs. You deserve better than that. Embarking on this journey shows that you want more for yourself and that in itself is praiseworthy!

Before I proceed, I'd like to reiterate a few words of caution. Firstly, if thinking back on painful times in your life causes you to feel extremely low, depressed, or makes you consider harming yourself in anyway, please seek professional advice and do not proceed until things have settled down. Secondly, and I cannot stress this enough, self exploration is not designed to make you *relive* your past experiences or feelings. You should, in no way, immerse yourself in or dwell on the past. Your focus should always be on yourself in the here and now. Your aim should be to improve things in your life as they are today, not to throw yourself back into painful parts of your younger years.

Remember: The past has passed. It cannot be changed. It can be enlightening to look back in order to discover how your early experiences informed your self beliefs; however, dwelling on the past can be unproductive and unnecessarily painful. Be kind to yourself and as you continue, remember to treat yourself like you would treat a friend.

Your Childhood

Childhood and adolescence were the times in your life when you did most of your learning, but this learning was not restricted to the hours you spent in school each day! Rather, nearly everything you experienced in your childhood taught you something. You were a blank slate, a sponge soaking up everything going on around you. During your early years you learned about rules and restrictions, cause and effect. You learned how to protect yourself in the physical world by accidentally hurting yourself or witnessing other people getting hurt. You began to understand more about other people; how your actions could affect them and how theirs in turn, could affect you. Your early experiences in your family home and your first few years in school helped you develop a broader understanding of human emotions. You developed expectations for yourself and the people around you. Your relationships with your primary care givers, siblings, and extended family, helped you develop a relationship pattern, or *blueprint*, that would later inform both your instincts and actions when beginning and maintaining relationships throughout your life.

For example, if you were often neglected as a small child, you may have become exceedingly independent and/or untrusting of other people. If you were raised in a secure and loving environment, you may have grown up to be optimistic, confident, and easy going in relationships. If you were raised in a family in which you played the role of 'scapegoat' you may have gone through life always believing that you were at fault when things went wrong, even if the event had little or nothing to do with you. The type of household you grew up in informed what you understood to be *normal* and therefore shaped who you grew up to be.

Throughout your school days your horizons broadened beyond life at home. You began to see the world through the eyes of your teachers and other children. You learned about different ways of living when you visited the homes of your friends. Your understanding of the world and humanity itself continued to expand when you were faced with other people's opinions and beliefs. You may have become more aware of the things that made you and your family unique. Even something as simple as noticing the differences between mealtimes in your home versus those in a friend's home challenged your understanding of what you experienced as normal. It can be argued that every single aspect of your childhood is relevant to who you grew up to be. From things as simple as your birth order to any extreme or unique experiences you may have had growing up, the life you lived as a child is part of who are now. However, this does not mean that your present and future experiences will be forever molded by the things you experienced as a child! It is very important to remember that.

Nor does it mean that you cannot grow out of damaging behavioral patterns or harmful personality traits. Having had a difficult childhood does not mean that you are bound to have a difficult adulthood. On the contrary, human beings have an incredible ability to heal and grow far beyond where they began. The human intellect and emotional spectrum can continue expanding throughout our entire lives, meaning that, although your unique childhood is inherently part of you, you will always have the capability to change and grow past it. And what's really wonderful is that by seeking to learn from your early experiences, you can use them to fuel your future accomplishments.

Human beings - like many other species - are born into groups. Whether you were born into a family of two or a family of twenty-five, it is within this group that you acquired (or did not acquire) your basic human needs. You learned about yourself and the world around you through play, receiving affection and protection, and watching your parents and siblings make their way through life. You learned who to depend on for food and shelter. You learned how to keep yourself safe from harm. But if one or more of your fundamental needs were not met in your early days, you may have missed out on some vital education about self protection and self preservation. This could mean that, in your adulthood, you are still lacking those important skills. Have a look at the following outline to familiarize yourself with ten fundamental human needs that shaped who you were as a child and who you are today.

Our Needs and How To Get Them

1.) Physical and Emotional Upkeep

This encompasses your most basic physical human needs such as food, clothing, shelter, and rest. It also includes your basic emotional needs such as being listened to and valued, having others respect your feelings and opinions, being understood by those close to you, and feeling as though you were properly cared for. If these basic human needs were not met by your primary caregiver as a child, it will likely have had an effect on your life as an adult. For instance, if your physical needs were neglected by your parents you may have developed a tendency to steal or hide food. You may have developed a tendency to not care for yourself properly or to care for yourself in extremely independent ways. You might be wary of accepting help from others or you may be highly dependent on it.

Being emotionally neglected in childhood can have some very serious effects on you in adulthood. Having your parents neglect your emotional needs may have included being ignored as a child, being given little or no choices in life, being taunted or ridiculed, having your feelings negated, being called *naughty* or *bad* when you were simply trying to be heard or noticed, or never being asked how you felt. Adults who did not have their emotional needs met as children may grow up to be unsure of themselves or believe that their feelings don't matter.

They may not be able to identify or trust their own feelings or self-beliefs or they may feel responsible or guilty for things they have no control over. As you might imagine, adults that fall into this category are likely to experience depression and/or low self-esteem to some degree. They may have trouble self-soothing or overcoming negative emotions. They may be more emotionally sensitive than their peers. They may develop habits of self harm or neglect. They are also more likely to end up with personality disorders and have a hard time maintaining relationships.

It's important to note that these basic needs do not stop at childhood. As adults, our needs are much the same and it's surprising how many of us neglect them. Often these things can get lost in a daily life that is packed with too much physical or mental work. If your life is particularly busy (whether that's due to work, your family, or an overly rigorous fitness routine), it's likely that you could be missing out on the sleep and nutrition your body and mind need.

Furthermore, getting enough rest and attending to your emotional needs might go by the wayside if you're too busy focusing on other things. It's important to remember that your physical and emotional upkeep is just as important as everything else on your to-do list. Make sure that you take time to rest in your daily life and avoid skipping meals where possible. Put due focus on your emotional wellbeing by practicing good self care and indulging in quiet time. Learn to listen to your feelings and make yourself a priority.

2.) Security and Protection

Human beings have an innate need to feel a sense of safety and security throughout their lives. As babies, it is the responsibility of our mother or primary caregiver to keep us safe from harm. This comes in the form of providing us with a secure home and making sure we have a guardian looking after us until we are old enough to protect ourselves. But it's not just having a lock on the door that keeps us safe. Our parents are also responsible for teaching us to steer clear of danger. They teach us survival skills like how to swim, how to be street smart, and what to do in an emergency. They teach us not to touch things that might burn us, not to bother sleeping dogs, and more importantly, how to stay safe among our peers. Being raised without due emphasis placed on our security and protection could lead us to get into more danger than other children. If a child does not feel safe at home, either because they are being abused or their safety is being neglected, their sense of security will be disrupted. This could lead them to have similar security issues and phobias throughout their life.

In adulthood, ensuring we have a sense of security and protection includes things like having a good healthcare plan, financial security, living in a safe and secure building, and protecting ourselves emotionally. Feeling unsafe or insecure in any way can lead to extreme stress, fear, and anxiety. Feelings of insecurity in relationships can lead a person to have myriad problematic relationships or to steer clear of intimacy entirely.

3.) Social Stimulation

Human beings are social creatures by nature. Much of our physical and emotional wellbeing is closely tied to social interaction. We are pack animals who thrive when surrounded by people who care about us and offer us support. Be they family or friends, classmates or colleagues, having a forum to give and receive attention is necessary for our intellectual stimulation and our overall wellbeing. Having regular contact with friends and family means getting support when you need it. This is especially important when it comes to dealing with major life changes such as losing a job or a loved one, or coping with serious illness. Furthermore, humans respond exceedingly well to shared social situations including enjoying time with friends, having regular meetings with people who have the same interests as you, or getting involved in support groups to meet people who have similar struggles as you.

Having a forum to share and discuss our feelings can lead to faster recovery when times are hard. By talking to family and friends about our problems, we can reduce stress and increase feelings of positivity and confidence. A life lacking in contact with others can lead to isolation, depression, ill health, and difficulties such as social discomfort or inappropriate social behavior. Without having a social outlet or proper support system, you may experience increased stress, increased risk of substance abuse, and decreased self-esteem.

4.) Intimacy, Love, and Affection

Close relationships with other people play a hugely significant role in the lives of humans. We are born with a *need* to love and be loved. From the day we are born and throughout our childhood, our parents and guardians are responsible for providing us with love that is both selfless and unconditional. It is this aspect of the relationships we had with our parents in childhood that contributes the most when it comes to out intimate relationships in adulthood. For instance, if your mother was not warm or affectionate with you as a child, you may have grown up finding it hard to give or receive warmth and affection where others were concerned.

Furthermore, if the love you received from your mother or father was *conditional* - that is to say you found yourself constantly striving for their attention and/or believing that nothing you did was ever good enough where they were concerned - you may find that your intimate relationships in adulthood take on a similar shape. You may find it hard to accept love from other people because you've never believed yourself to be worthy of it. You may find yourself repeating negative patterns in your love life.

For instance, imagine that you grew up in a family where you were constantly vying for your mother's love but nothing you did was ever good enough to receive it. In this instance, you may have developed a pattern of dating people who are cold or emotionally unavailable; people who you have to chase or try unreasonably hard to impress. You may recognize that you date people who are rude, abusive, or emotionally shut down. Alternatively you might find that you run from relationships where love is too *easy* to achieve. Where love is readily available, you may lose interest or become emotionally shut down yourself.

Growing up with healthy, loving relationships at home presents a stable opportunity for us to give and receive respect, support, laughter, affection and care. It allows us to trust others more easily and makes it easier to accept positive feelings that other people have for us. If you grew up in a household with two parents who regularly displayed positive aspects of love - that is, they were affectionate with one another, they showed each other mutual respect, they shared responsibilities equally, et cetera - this would've created a healthy template from which you would've learned the importance and positive sides of romantic love.

On the contrary, if your parents' relationship was abusive, one-sided, or nonexistent, you may have grown up feeling wary of love entirely. Romantic love offers a forum for sensuality, privacy, and intimacy. Love itself is a fundamental need that is found in many species, and in the case of humans, it is one that reiterates the importance of our existence in groups. In childhood, having affectionate and respectful relationships with one's primary caregiver, siblings, and friends sets us up for having equally healthy relationships as adults. Our early experiences with intimate love help us learn how to navigate our romantic love lives as adults.

Remember, growing up in a family in which you did not receive this fundamental need is not a prophecy of having a similarly loveless adulthood. Although our early experiences do inform many of our beliefs and behaviors, we can overcome them. Taking the time to recognize your patterns with love and trying to understanding where they originated is like arming yourself against your instinct to follow the same pattern in years to come. Identifying your negative patterns is the first step toward putting a stop to them.

5.) A Feeling of Identity and Importance

It is extremely important for human beings to feel valued and to feel as though they have a purpose. Much of how we feel about ourselves is tied up in how we view ourselves in light of the world around us. Identity as a fundamental need is inclusive of two parts. The first pertains to ourselves as a single entity, while the second pertains to ourselves within a group to which we belong. Once again, the idea that humans are pack animals who work best within tribes stresses the importance of being part of a group. This doesn't always have to come in the form of being part of a large family or a close knit group of friends. Group identity can come from your profession, your political beliefs, your age, your interests, and virtually anything else you identify with wherein you are not the only one.

For instance, any statement that ties you to a group of people, i.e. I am a democrat... a vegetarian... a doctor... a football enthusiast. Things like these which tie us to other human beings create a sense of belonging that is vital to how we view ourselves in the world. A sense of importance can be formed within these groups as well if they include systems of hierarchy and reward.

For instance, you may be the one who is responsible for organizing your football team or you may be the president of a certain club you to belong to. You may have something - a possession, a talent, or a skill - that is valued within your group. That sense of importance within your group increases your feelings of belonging while feeding your sense of individual identity.

Your sense of identity and importance also exists outside of groups. When you eventually separated from your mother after being physically joined together via pregnancy and breastfeeding, you began developing your own individuality. Your ideas, feelings, and needs became your own. Most importantly, when you were young you developed beliefs about your own *value* both in relation to the role you played within your family and you existence as an individual.

As a child, these beliefs about your individual value were founded in both how well you functioned in groups as well as how you did on your own. As a child you were, in many ways, reliant on other people to help you develop a sense of individual value. You acquired it by receiving respect, guidance, and praise from school teachers, family members, and peers. For instance, if you grew up feeling valued and respected by others, you will have been more likely to continue owning that sense of value into your adulthood (where your need for validation from others would have decreased).

However, if you grew up receiving little to no validation from others you are more likely to continue to seek it in your adulthood. You may rely on others to tell you when you have done something well; you may need them to encourage you or cheer you on. For someone with an unstable sense of self - that is, one who struggles to see the value they possess - this could mean not only undervaluing themselves but also growing up to be highly sensitive when it comes to coping with rejection and criticism.

Knowing that you are important and having a strong sense of identity and belonging plays a large role in your self-esteem. It helps you trust your own decisions and ideas. It means being less swayed by others. It could even mean the difference between living a clean lifestyle and falling into habits of substance abuse and poor self care. Wanting to feel valued, important, loved, and wanted is not something to be embarrassed about; rather, it is a fundamental need which all humans possess.

6.) Play

It's true. Humans, and many other species, have a fundamental need for play and leisure! In childhood and adolescence, play prepares you for adulthood by teaching you how to communicate, understand others, and protect yourself in social situations. As babies and young children, it is important for our mothers or primary caregivers to take the time to play with us. Playful interaction between mother and child not only teaches communication and skills for life, but it also increases the maternal bond, thus creating feelings of safety and security. During this time in our lives, the more our mother is available to us and the more concerned she is with our needs, the more we will feel that we can depend on her for direction, protection, and love.

Furthermore we learn through this relationship the consequences of our actions, how to please other people, and what behaviors receive the most response. It is within this primary attachment relationship that we develop the instincts and patterns that we will carry with us into every other relationship in our lives. On an evolutionary level, it is in the best interest of both mother and child to explore and practice appropriate social behavior together for the survival of our species. If a mother neglects her childs need to interact in this manner - and in effect, remains detached from her child - the child may lose out on some important lessons regarding socialization, self importance, and both physical and emotional survival.

But play isn't just important for children, it is also an important part of adulthood. A life that lacks recreation can lead to depression, stress, and resentfulness. It can make us feel detached from other people and the world around us. Leisure is important for stress relief, physical health and wellbeing, and our overall enjoyment of life. It can prevent burnout, boredom, and chronic fatigue, not to mention playing an important part in maintaining healthy friendships and loving relationships. Furthermore, as individuals all of us have a need for lightness and fun.

If you have a demanding career or a stressful home life, it can be hard to make time for yourself. It seems that when our lives are very busy and we're stretched for time, play is often the first thing to go. If this is the case in your life, try to restructure your days so that you can dedicate some time to recreation. You will find that the more you smile and laugh in life, the more you 'play' with your friends and family, the better you will feel both inside and out.

7.) Personal Growth

The human brain is designed for curiosity, creativity, and problem solving. Focusing on personal growth, education, and self-exploration feeds your feelings of positive self-worth and keeps the mind from become bored, stagnant, or complacent. So too, personal development helps us to realistically evaluate our skills and set appropriate goals for ourselves. Personal growth is something we need to engage in throughout our lives. Continuing to expand your knowledge and your horizons throughout your life will not only keep you intellectually stimulated, it will also increase your feelings of self-confidence and earn you the respect of others.

When we don't spend enough time on personal growth, we are placing less importance on ourselves than we deserve. In effect, we are giving up on ever becoming more than we are today. Imagine having someone you love telling you that you have no chance of ever progressing in life. Imagine them telling you that there's no use in ever trying to be better than you are right now. How would that make you feel? When you cease to grow and change - to seek new knowledge and skills - you are actively telling yourself that you're not worth anymore than what you have today.

Personal growth comes in many forms. Everything from learning new practical skills to understanding ourselves better on a psychological level helps us learn to make smart choices and positive changes in our lives. When it comes to self-esteem, a lack of personal growth can be detrimental. If we don't spend enough time furthering our knowledge and skills, we can hardly expect to progress very far in our careers or our relationships with others. Furthermore, a lack of personal growth can cause us to feel insecure, insignificant, useless, or hopeless. It can rob you of your sense of purpose and importance. Concentrating on personal growth means giving yourself opportunities to be your best self, to reach your goals and live up to your full potential.

When you were a child, if your parents and teachers didn't place enough emphasis on personal growth or if they failed to recognize your true potential, you may have in turn, learned to do the same. You may have failed to study or progress very far in school. You may have held yourself back from trying new things or perfecting skills you had a natural talent for. You may have declined opportunities that could've earned you respect or lead you to success.

Chances are, if you developed a habit of ignoring your strengths and potential as a child, you probably continue to do so in adulthood. Alternatively by rarely seeking personal growth or reaching goals that were set for you as a child, you may have grown up to be an impatient adult; one who regularly gives up or quits when results are not easily reached.

For example, you may have a strong desire to learn a certain skill but you may lack perseverance when you faced with the opportunity to learn it. You may quit when the going gets tough. When faced with obstacles you may be quick to resign yourself to the belief that overcoming it is impossible. Without allowing yourself to overcome difficulties in life, you're holding yourself back from experiencing the many positive effects of personal growth. In this light you can imagine how being the type of person who regularly 'gives up' could drive your self-esteem into the ground. So too, allowing the mind to stagnate is bound to make you feel lethargic and *stuck* in life. If this is the case for you, try to think of personal growth as a gift, not a chore.

8.) Participation and Community

A fundamental need for participation and community provides further evidence of the pack mentality of human beings and our basic need to be a part of something bigger than ourselves. Earlier I discussed our need for identity and importance and how it functions in both an individual sense and in a group sense. Within groups, we have the opportunity to give and receive help from others. We can use our own strengths and expertise from our own lives to affect others positively.

When we help other people, we are actively feeding our feelings of value and positive self worth. When we receive help from others, we gain feelings of importance, support, and community. Similarly, working together with other people toward reaching a unified goal increases our feelings of belonging and security. Participating in groups at work or school, or joining clubs, community projects and sports teams can strengthen your capacity for cooperation, communication, receptiveness to others, and sense of responsibility for something bigger than yourself.

As children, having a voice within a group is an important way for us to learn the value of our opinions as well as how to compromise and effectively reach group wide decisions. When a child is part of a family or group in which their voice is heard and their opinions are valued, they are more likely to develop the confidence they will later need in order to trust themselves and be a valued member of groups in their adulthood. This will be particularly useful to them when it comes to joining the working world.

Similarly, when children participate with other children, they have opportunities to practice skills they will need later in life. Group participation in both childhood and adulthood is vitally important when it comes to combatting feelings of isolation, worthlessness and loneliness. Being part of almost any type of group means achieving that vital sense of belonging we all need. Participation and a sense of community can give your life more purpose and meaning.

9.) Control

The human mind requires a certain amount of control to stave off the effects of chaos on our emotional wellbeing. A person who has very little control in their life could develop stress induced illnesses, depression, obsessive compulsive disorder, and/or general malaise. When we are in situations in which we have no control, it can be hard to summon a sense of security or mastery over our own lives. When thrust into situations where we can't predict an outcome or we are powerless against a certain force, we can experience strong feelings of fear, uneasiness, anxiety and feelings of impending doom. Every individual needs to have control over something, whether that thing is their career, love life, hobbies, health, or simply their own thoughts.

Our feelings about control and how it functions in our lives often relates directly to our childhood experiences. Children who live in unstable households are often starved of the control they need in order to grow up to be secure adults. This is particularly true for those who come from homes where one or both parents are alcoholics or where any of their basic needs are not being appropriately met. If for instance, a child is left alone a lot or is forced to fend for himself rather than being properly taken care of, he may be in a near constant state of nervousness or fear for his own safety.

Similarly, if a child feels that he cannot trust his parents to control the world around him - if for instance one or both parents are emotionally unstable, his home life is particularly chaotic or his environment rapidly changing - he may be reluctant to trust other people throughout his life.

If a person is starved of control or disallowed the right of choice, it can be argued that they will be more prone to self-doubt and low self-esteem throughout their lives. A number of cognitive difficulties are believed to be caused by an ungratified need for control. These include eating disorders, anxiety and mood disorders, and obsessive compulsive disorder. Individuals who have more opportunities to make important decisions and who have a higher degree of choice over their lives are likely to feel more confident and have a better quality of life.

10.) Freedom

Every individual has a need for freedom in their life. This need spans across many parts of our lives and includes freedom of speech, thoughts and ideas, having a right to your own passion and interests, and feeling free to take your own path in life. Freedom also refers to an individuals need for autonomy, choice, education, and risk taking. This is relevant to us in an individual sense, but also affects us within our communities and close relationships. A life lacking in freedom can be stifling, frustrating, and unfulfilling. It can cause anxiety and make you feel like you have no control over your surroundings. If allowed to go unnoticed or unidentified, an absence of freedom can also lead to harmful behavior and/or dysfunctional relationships.

As a child, if you weren't allowed to make choices for yourself or you were discouraged from exploring the world around you, you may have grown up to be fearful or highly dependent on others. A lack of freedom in childhood could also have led you into patterns of rule breaking or rebellion. If your family, friends, or teachers were over protective or highly critical of you, you may have felt discouraged from doing the things you wanted to do.

Being bullied in school or at home could've robbed you of the freedom you needed to explore the world on your own terms and become the person you wanted to be. Similarly, if your parents didn't allow you to explore your own interests - if, for instance they forced you into a path that suited their desires more than yours - your feelings of freedom may have been compromised. You may have grown up feeling as though you lacked autonomy.

If you grew up without a sense of personal freedom, it's possible that you may have created certain habits and feelings that followed you into your adulthood. You may have a tendency to hold yourself back from following your true interests or you might be afraid of standing out in a crowd. A lack of freedom in your childhood could have caused you to have a hard time prioritizing yourself as an adult or carving out time that's just for you. You may struggle to be assertive with your thoughts and feelings.

If you were overprotected as a child you may have developed a fear of trying new things or taking risks. But a life lacking in freedom may have also led you down paths that are dangerous or self-destructive. If you developed rebellious tendencies due to a lack of freedom in your childhood, you may struggle with drug or alcohol addiction as an adult or find it hard to hold down a job. You might be more likely to choose the road less travelled rather than follow the beaten path.

Exercise #5

Basic human needs are an integral part of our physical and psychological wellbeing but if your needs were neglected in your early days, you may be experiencing the effects in your adulthood. You may regularly neglect your basic needs in your adulthood or may have developed patterns of self destruction, self loathing, problematic relationships, resentment or bitterness, and difficulty prioritizing yourself above others. If you are in the habit of ignoring your own basic needs, your self-esteem may be suffering as a result.

Begin this exercise by looking back over the list of basic human needs and identify any that were lacking in your childhood to any degree.

Ask yourself the following questions:

Did you have all the food, clothing, and shelter you required? Did you feel safe and protected at home? Was your health looked after?

Did your primary caregivers value and respect you? Were they attentive? Did they encourage you to have your own opinions or were you regularly dismissed by them?

Did you have regular social stimulation? Were you encouraged to speak your mind? Were you able to maintain friendships?

How would you describe your early experiences with love? Were you given plenty of love, support, and affection in your family home? Were you in equal and respectful relationships?

Were you made to feel important and special as a child? Were you compared to others or valued for who you were? Did your primary caregivers take an interest in you and your future?

Did you have plenty of opportunities to play and let loose? Did your parents and siblings play with you or were you often left alone?

Were you offered plenty of opportunities to be creative and grow as a person? Were you encouraged to learn and delve into your own interests or were you only encouraged to do what others believed was best for you? Was your personal growth ignored or taken for granted?

Did you have enough control as a child? Were your primary caregivers neglectful or over protective? Was your household particularly chaotic or lacking in routine? Were you given plenty of opportunities for choice?

Did you have freedom for self-exploration and risk taking? Were you respected for being autonomous or were you made to follow in someone else's footsteps?

Once you've answered these questions, look over the list again and identify anything that is missing or limited in your life *today*.

Can you identify any similarities or patterns?
Do you recognize a correlation between who you were as a child and who you are today?

Taking time to look into how or why you developed certain personality traits and patterns in life will help you understand them better. Once you understand why things are the way they are, you can start to challenge them and change the things you're unhappy with. Remember, self-exploration like this may be emotionally activating. Be kind to yourself during this process and don't push yourself too hard!

Your past is not who you are, it's simply where you've been.

You and Your Family: Leaving Behind The Past, Building Healthy Relationships

As you discovered in that last section, how you feel and who you are today is often a reflection of your childhood experiences. Similarly, your relationship patterns could be deeply rooted in your early attachment relationships. There are many circumstances and external forces that could have caused you to have negative self beliefs as a child and many of these may have followed you into your adulthood. In your childhood home, every family member had their own role(s) to play. Whether you were in family of two or ten, whether you played one role or four. Your birth order, living conditions, the health and emotional stability of your caretakers, and the relationships you had with your siblings all contributed to the role you played within your family.

Most of us take our childhood roles with us when we transition into adulthood. In a way, they function as a foundation upon which your entire sense of self rests. The roles you played in your childhood relationships are likely to be repeated to some extent in the roles you play in those of your adulthood. For instance, if you grew up feeling wary of authority, you may struggle in work environments as an adult. If you were often blamed when things went wrong as a child, you might still feel at fault in similar situations in adulthood whether this is true or not.

For a child to grow up happy, healthy, and emotionally secure, their household should be a supportive, safe, and respectful environment. This means being encouraged to develop their own strengths and personality traits as well as having their thoughts and opinions valued. It means being raised in a home where all family members are considerate of one another and each respects the value of the others. In such an environment, a person's self worth springs from being supported *(in both the physical and emotional sense)*, being appropriately encouraged, and receiving praise when it is due.

Unfortunately, not all family relationships are positive and supportive. In many households children are given too much responsibility, too little respect, and/or no support at all. If a child is raised in a household where things are chaotic or unsafe, they might develop some harmful survival skills. Although these habits may help them cope with the lack of control in their life, they could also cause anxiety, obsessive tendencies, and feelings of low self worth.

A child with too much responsibly might be forced to take care of herself, her siblings, and be in charge of other responsibilities better suited to an adult. Situations like these may be caused by sick, negligent, or alcoholic parents. A child in a situation like this could miss out on valuable childhood experiences as well as some of their basic human needs. They may grow up to be needy, co-dependent, overly focused on caring for others, or emotionally immature.

It is important to recognize that even the slightest unrest in childhood can have an effect on how we feel about ourselves in relation to the world around us. It isn't only children from broken homes that are affected by their early experiences. Many individuals grow up in homes that are relatively normal yet they still come up slightly deficient in one or more basic needs, causing them to develop unhealthy habits and harmful relationships patterns.

A child who is not cared for properly, or whose early relationships are unstable could easily develop low self-esteem among a variety of other difficulties in life. This is particularly interesting when it comes to children who are responsible for the wellbeing of others within their household.

For instance, a child with a sick or absent parent may be entirely competent when it comes to feeding himself and his siblings, but regardless of how well he may cope with this added responsibility, he still requires protection, security, and emotional support from his parents. He needs the freedom to learn and grow through his early social experiences and in order to do so, his life at home must provide the appropriate security he needs to safely explore the world around him. If a child is raised by an incapable parent they may be forced to grow up too soon causing detriment to their emotional wellbeing in the future.

Along similar lines, if a younger child is being cared for by an older sibling, they too will miss out on valuable life lessons. Without a solid adult role model this child's experience is likely to lack in security and structure. He might not learn how to identify his feelings or effectively communicate his needs. He may struggle with anxiety or tantrums. He might have difficulties making and maintaining friendships or grow up without the ability to prioritize his own needs.

Every individual needs to feel valued and appreciated. Every child needs respect and love. Unfortunately, there are many circumstances that could prevent a child from receiving the support they need. The following list shows some common circumstances that may cause children to miss out in life.

Children Who Miss Out

1.) Children of Alcoholics

Children who grow up in alcoholic homes are often put under high amounts of pressure, stress, and responsibility. They live in environments that are chaotic, unpredictable, or in constant flux. These children may come across as highly emotional, desperate for attention, or oddly mature for their age. Their relationships with family members are often unstable and lack the trust and security they require. A child living with an alcoholic parent may feel desperate for love and attention from them. They may develop extreme behaviors such as screaming and crying, self harming, or becoming completely withdrawn. This child might feel like they have to be constantly on guard.

They may be scared, anxious, or feel like they have to be extra cautious around their parents. And very often they will grow up believing that they are at fault for their parents' actions. For instance, a parent who is highly critical of their child or verbally abusive when they're drinking, could drive a child into dangerously low feelings of self worth. The child may develop low self-esteem and depression as a result. They may try to alter their behavior constantly in the hopes of avoiding a parent's drunken rage or insult.

Due to the unstable nature of alcoholic homes, a child may develop unhealthy relationship patterns that they inevitably repeat throughout their lives. Children of alcoholics are often neglected and may grow up with a tendency to seek constant approval from others. Their understanding of love may be entirely skewed meaning that they may act as either victim, rescuer, or antagonist in future relationships. Children of alcoholics may have a hard time relaxing and enjoying life. They may grow up to be nervous, scared of conflict, and unable to cope with criticism. They may seek to please other people on a constant but may struggle to accept praise or thanks for their actions. They may develop obsessive compulsive disorder or struggle with other control issues.

Unfortunately, one of the most common outcomes for children who are raised by alcoholics is growing up to struggle with alcohol and drug addiction themselves. It's important to recognize if you have inherited your alcoholic parent's damaging personality traits or behavior in order to grow beyond your past and build a brighter future for yourself.

2.) Children with Physically or Mentally Ill Parents

Similar to children of alcoholic parents, children living with a physically or mentally unwell parent may also regularly find themselves in positions of responsibility. Having to care for ones' parents and/or siblings due to the parent being unfit creates an environment where the child is forced to suppress their own needs and behave like an adult. If a parent is mentally ill - with or without a clear diagnosis - the child is likely to develop unhealthy survival skills to help them cope with the chaos around them. Living in an environment that is rapidly changing means that the child will lack structure and security. A child might feel like they have to walk on egg shells so as not to upset their parent. Alternatively, if the parent is suffering from extreme bouts of depression, the child may feel responsible or as though they are at fault.

This can lead the child to struggle with guilt complexes later in life as well as tendencies to obsessively organize and/or 'prepare for the worst' at all times. Children with mentally ill parents are likely to grow up putting their own needs last, being constantly alert to any changes in their parent's mood or behavior, keeping secrets or lying about household conditions, and protecting siblings from harm. Children in these situations may grow up to have low self-esteem manifesting in fear of conflict, co-dependent relationships, difficulties trusting other people, and difficulty prioritizing their own needs.

Children whose parents are *physically* unwell may also be placed under heightened levels of stress and given too much responsibility; however, they may not be subjected to a household which is necessarily chaotic. A child in this situation may learn to suppress feelings of fear and sadness in an attempt to cope with the difficult situation at home. They may act like the 'clown' or the 'caretaker' of the family. They may act out at school or have trouble identifying their feelings. Alternatively, they may shut down completely or become angry or aggressive.

Sadly, the needs of these children may be brushed aside or misunderstood at home while the sick parent's health takes priority. Children in situations like these may grow up feeling insignificant or under par. They may have trouble identifying their own needs versus the needs of those around them. They may suffer from anxiety, panic attacks, or feelings of impending doom. Similar patterns may follow them into adulthood.

3.) Children with Sick or Disabled Siblings

Children living with a chronically ill sibling may be subjected to regular disruption in their daily lives which can lead to emotional instability and feelings of low self worth. This child may feel forced to look after or protect their sibling, often taking a 'backseat' within the family. If a child in this situation is not given the appropriate care and attention they require during this time, they may struggle to understand what is happening to their sibling and what it means for them.

They may have difficulties navigating their feelings, thus suppressing their negative emotions or acting out in school or at home. This child may grow up believing that they are at fault for their siblings illness. If they aren't receiving enough care and attention from their parents, they may have tantrums or seek negative attention, often acting as though they too, are sick.

If the sick sibling passes away, some children experience intense feelings of guilt, often known as *survivor guilt*. In extreme circumstances like this, grieving parents may fail to recognize the effect the death has had on the surviving sibling. So too, if the parents fail to recover from an event like this or they fall into serious bouts of depression, the surviving sibling is likely to feel and act as though their entire foundation has been shaken. Their daily life may take on a whole new shape during the period of transition following the death. Things in the household may become unpredictable or unstable. A child in such a household could easily develop care-taking behaviors, fear of disaster, anxiety and panic attacks, feelings of guilt and unimportance, and/or a chronic sense of hopelessness or pessimism. In adulthood they may struggle to prioritize their own needs and may find it hard to find the bright side in life. They may have little faith in themselves or expect the worst in a variety of avenues in life.

4.) Children with Narcissistic Parents

Growing up with a narcissistic parent can make a child feel invisible. Narcissistic parents act like the Sun in the universe of the home. They are extremely self-focused, often failing to form healthy attachments to others, including their children. They may be incapable of recognizing when they are to blame, opting instead, to blame their children or partners when things go wrong. These parents may be cold or unaffectionate. They may be childish or immature and may always play the victim in times of conflict. As such, children of narcissistic parents often do not receive the nurture and care they require. They may lack a suitable role model from whom they can learn how to make and maintain healthy relationships for themselves.

Furthermore, a child living with a narcissistic parent may try endlessly and desperately to secure the love of their parent to no avail. They are likely to experience bullying, rejection, abuse, neglect, shaming, name calling, violence, and/or indifference from their narcissistic parent, making it likely for them to grow up being emotionally scarred or unstable in some way.

Children who live in their narcissistic parent's shadow are highly likely to develop problems with their self-esteem. The more the parent ignores the child's achievements, the less the child will believe in their own abilities. Without attention and praise from her parent, the child often feels like she is not 'good enough' or that she can't do anything right. She learns to doubt herself and her beliefs and struggles to trust herself in many avenues in life. She may think of herself as unloveable.

Unfortunately, children of narcissistic parents often have their struggles go unnoticed by teachers and other adult family members, especially if the child comes from what appears to be a 'good home'. They may exhibit similar behavior to their parent, making it difficult for them to maintain relationships of their own. These children may unknowingly develop behaviors that are hurtful toward or unaccepting of others. They may have trouble compromising and struggle to understand other people's perspectives. Children of narcissistic parents tend to judge themselves too harshly and often fail to recognize why their relationships (including friendships and other familial relationships) don't last.

They may be defensive, overly sensitive, and find it extremely hard to cope with criticism. If the relationship between child and parent is particularly tumultuous and the child never receives the acceptance they crave from their parent, they will likely develop a habit of entering relationships with people who are similarly critical of them and/or hard to get close to. They may develop a habit of 'chasing' people who reject them and become extremely emotional or depressed when a relationship ends, even if it was short lived.

Overcoming a childhood such as this can be hard but it is not an impossible feat. Learning to recognize what patterns you have developed as a result of your childhood is the first step towards making changes in your adulthood. It is important for people in these circumstances to learn how to build themselves up so that they can withstand moments of rejection or failure without descending into depression or harmful behavior.

5.) Victims of Abuse or Neglect

Children who are treated poorly by their primary caregivers often grow up feeling like second class citizens in their own homes. There are many types of abuse and although each has its own specific symptoms and outcomes, most abused children grow up to have a depleted self esteem which relies heavily on the approval others. Abused children are often forced to grow up long before they're ready to and this means behaving in ways that often isolate themselves from other children. They may be secretive, nervous, or wary of people who show an interest in them. They may be aggressive or disruptive. They may be highly emotional and have trouble distinguishing between positive and negative attention.

In addition to receiving damaging and dangerous treatment from their parents, abused children may also be regularly forced to lie in order to keep the family secret. They may therefore experience feelings of shame, fear, sadness, loneliness, and hopelessness. If a child becomes used to hiding their true feelings, they may find it equally hard to express their emotions as adults. Many children of abuse grow up to feel worthless or subpar in some way. They may find it hard to let people get close to them or they may be suspicious of the intentions of others. It is also possible that these children will grow up to be abusers themselves in one way or another. If this is the case it is of upmost importance that they learn more constructive ways to express their feelings so that the cycle of abuse will not continue into future generations.

Overcoming an abusive past can be very difficult. Not only is it hard to revisit difficult events in your life, but even so much as admitting what happened to you as a child can feel like climbing an emotional

Everest. Children who grew up hiding their feelings often continue doing so throughout their lives. They may struggle with self doubt and find it extremely hard to trust other people. Their self-esteem and feelings of self worth can be dangerously low and may take a long time to recover.

Whereas people are often able to recognize when they have been a victim of abuse, identifying if you have been *neglected* as a child can be harder to recognize, especially in the case of emotional neglect. A child who is being neglected may struggle to understand what is happening to them, believing that the shortcoming is not their parents', but their own. Victims of child neglect often doubt their own experience because the signs and symptoms are harder to decipher than those of other types of abuse.

Similarly, teachers and extended family members often fail to recognize when a child's behavior is a product of being neglected at home. Neglected children may feel unhappy at home but often believe that they are the ones at fault. For instance, a child who is regularly ignored may grow up believing that they're not worthy of attention rather than understanding that they were let down by their parents.

A victim of abuse may have a tendency to get into, and remain in, other abusive relationships throughout their lives. Without being given the respect and love they needed as children, they may confuse abuse with love, thus seeking relationships with people who treat them poorly or who send mixed signals. Victims of abuse and neglect may find it hard trust themselves and other people. For this reason their behavior among peers can be misleading or confusing. They may struggle to allow people to get close to them. They be unusually private or suspicious of others.

On the other end of the spectrum, victims of abuse may have patterns of throwing themselves into new relationships wholeheartedly, becoming immediately attached to others and being devastated when things don't work out. These behaviors can present themselves in romantic relationships as well as with friends and co-workers. As adults, they may find it hard to motivate themselves or relax. They may regularly seek the approval of others or isolate themselves completely, and they often have a very hard time loving themselves.

6.) Children Whose Lives Lack Stability

There are many reasons a childs' life may lack stability. Some examples include low income households, households where one or both parents are unreliable, families who move around a lot, and families that are dysfunctional. Without a feeling of stability or security a child may find it difficult to socialize or develop healthy attachments to others. If the child comes from a low income household he may get bullied at school or completely isolate himself from other children, believing that he is unworthy of friendship or respect. Children from unstable homes may not receive the encouragement and support they need throughout their school days and may therefore abandon academia or other interests due to negative self beliefs and self doubt.

Furthermore, a child from an unstable home may be forced to take on too much responsibility within his family. For instance, if he is regularly left in charge of his younger siblings or forced to keep the household running while he is still emotionally immature, he may fail to recognize the importance of his school work or have difficulties socializing with other children. He may develop a tendency to abandon anything he's not immediately good at or indulge in dangerous or rebellious activities without being noticed.

A child in a tumultuous household might feel invisible, unimportant, or under valued while experiencing anxiety or a near constant fear that things could go wrong at any given moment. In an environment that is constantly changing - one in which the child lacks any control - he may miss out on valuable life lessons such as how to budget time and money or how to prioritize tasks. He may struggle with feelings of low self worth among his school mates or believe himself to be 'different' from everyone else, thus emotionally ostracizing himself from his peers. He may grow up to be highly emotional or unusually defensive. His low self-esteem could mean that he remains susceptible to behavior which is rebellious or dangerous throughout his life, unable to properly care for himself.

7.) Children of Deceased Parents

A child who has suffered the loss of a parent may develop a multitude of emotional disturbances including depression, anxiety, obsessive compulsive disorder, violent or aggressive behavior, isolated and introverted behavior, substance abuse and more. But often it's not just the loss of the deceased parent that causes these effects. Although grieving is extremely difficult for children to cope with, often things are made worse if their relationship with the surviving parent is unhealthy or unsupportive.

If the child is put in a position of responsibility rather than being taken care of during the grieving period, they may miss out on valuable experiences of personal growth, learning to overcome difficult situations, coping with negative emotions, and living beyond death. A sense of abandonment regarding either the deceased parent or the surviving one could lead to fear of further abandonment and rejection in adulthood.

As an adult, this person may shy away from close relationships. They may come across as guarded or exceedingly private and it's possible that they'll develop a pessimistic or morose outlook on life. Furthermore, a fear of death may hover over everything they do in life and as a result they might steer clear of risk taking or other ambitions. They may struggle to cope with negative beliefs about themselves and the world around them. They may never feel as though they have fully recovered from the loss of their parent.

8.) Children with Over Protective Parents

Parents who are over protective may cause their children to lose self confidence due to their own fears. A parent who is unusually focused on danger or consequence may prevent their child from indulging in experiences that are vital for their emotional and intellectual growth. They may never present opportunities for their children to overcome obstacles. Instead, they will encourage the child to steer clear of difficulty and danger entirely. Alternatively, the over protective parent my insist on doing everything for the child in an attempt at reducing risk.

Raising a child in an overbearing way can make it hard for them to believe in themselves and trust their own capabilities. Furthermore, when over protective parents steer their child away from social or physical challenges, the child may not gain the knowledge they would naturally acquire through experience. Although no parent wants their children to get hurt, there are certain things a child must learn from their own experience. For instance, living through conflict at school or among friends teaches us how to live through conflict in our adult relationships and at work.

People need to feel autonomous both as children and as adults. We need to learn to trust our instincts within relationships and the physical world. If the opportunity to develop this self trust is taken from us at a young age or if we are discouraged from making decisions in our own lives, we are unlikely to trust ourselves as adults. This could mean growing up to be needy or fearful in relationships.

Furthermore, a child who is physically over protected may struggle with a multitude of phobias, anxiety, and panic throughout their life. Being over protected can take away a child's opportunities for choice and control. It can make them feel like an extension of their parents rather than allowing them the independence and individuality they need. As an adult, struggling to achieve a sense of autonomy can have terrible effects on your self esteem. Learning to stand on your own two feet is difficult if you've rarely been allowed to do it. However, these difficulties can be overcome with some determination and dedication to yourself.

Exercise #6

Take a short amount of time to look back over the list above. Reflect briefly on any ideas that sounded familiar to you. Do not spend a large amount of time or energy on these things from your past. There is no use in forcing yourself to relive things that were hard enough the first time around. Rather, take some time to treat yourself kindly today. Think of this as giving your inner child the love and comfort they deserve. Think of it as starting to heal from some of your childhood wounds.

Make sure you do this exercise!

Whether you'd enjoy a nice hot bath or a long hike up a mountain, do something nice for yourself *TODAY*. Taking the time to self soothe is a necessary step in learning to love yourself. Being kind to yourself is an active way to tell yourself that you're worthy of happiness.

The Importance of Healthy Boundaries In Your Life

In that last section you saw many examples of situations that can lead a child into damaging behavior or low self-esteem. In many of these households the childs' life is lacking care and support, appropriate role models, and healthy boundaries. Many of these children are being forced to grow up too soon in one way or another. They are given too much or not enough responsibility. They are being neglected or unsupervised. They experience the weight of the world without being supported or correctly guided through grief and hardship.

These children may experiment with substance abuse, have unhealthy or inappropriate sexual relationships, or get into other dangerous activities as a result of their unstable upbringing. Their self-esteem may be so low that they cease to value their own lives or care for themselves at all. They may be exposed to adult problems before they are mature enough to handle them. Often, they will develop harmful relationship patterns that will continue to affect them negatively throughout life.

So what exactly are *'healthy boundaries'?* When we think about boundaries we might first think about physical boundaries: the way a mother keeps her child close to her in the presence of physical danger, the way we lock our doors at night to keep ourselves safe from theft or bodily harm, the way a playground might be fenced in to prevent roaming dogs from wandering in and attacking children. But what about psychological boundaries? What about the boundaries we need to protect us *emotionally*?

Human beings have a need for personal safety and security that goes far beyond the physical. We must know how to protect ourselves from emotional harm and psychological distress as well physical danger. We need boundaries to keep our relationships healthy, to help us express our thoughts and feelings without fear of ridicule, and to help us cope with difficult times.

A child who is raised with loving attention and a healthy set of boundaries is likely to fit easily into the world around them. They will grow up with a stable sense of self, an ability to accept and respect others, and a strong self-reliance that does not depend on the approval or protection of another. They will form strong bonds with others, experience lasting friendships, and understand the consequences of their actions. This person will be able to express their own needs and desires without fear of abandonment or rejection. Healthy boundaries are formed in households where children receive the security and safety they need from their parents. They are reinforced by feeling accepted and valued.

However, if a child's parents are unreliable or neglectful of their needs, they are likely to grow up with a warped understanding of healthy boundaries. They may not know how to protect themselves from emotional harm or even recognize when they are in emotionally dangerous territory. If children are starved of praise and guidance, they are likely to seek attention and approval in inappropriate or dangerous ways.

Adults who were abused or neglected as children often possess an underlying or subconscious dislike of themselves. Abuse after all, has the power to break a person down and make them feel worthless. The same can be said for children who are neglected, bullied, undervalued, ignored, or unloved. I have mentioned relationship patterns a number of times so far in this book and it's important to note that the ability to create healthy boundaries plays an integral role in the health of our relationships. In order to maintain healthy relationships with others (including relationships at work, with friends, and with our family members), we must know how to create psychological boundaries. This way, both us and the people around us will feel respected and safe.

A person who struggles to create boundaries might be thought of as a 'push over' or a 'soft touch. They may be extremely compromising. They might allow people to push past them on a busy sidewalk or cut in front of them while driving. This person may also be incredibly generous, always thinking about other people first and placing their own needs and desires at the bottom of their list of priorities. You might be wondering what could be so bad about being generous and kind? And the fact is, there's nothing *wrong* with generosity at all!

However, if a person's self esteem is so low that they struggle to create the boundaries they need to keep them emotionally safe, they may be opening themselves up to certain hardships without even knowing it. For instance, this person might allow themselves to be the butt of every joke or let people ridicule them for their opinions. They may allow themselves to be abused or taken advantage of by the people they love. They may have a tendency to cling to people who mistreat them. And most often they struggle to be assertive, thus rarely stating their own individual needs and feelings.

In order to create healthy boundaries for ourselves we have to be able to state our needs to people with whom we are in relationships. We need to feel as though our opinions matter and as though we are emotionally safe. Without healthy boundaries a person may not be able to express negative emotions to their co-workers, friends, or loved ones. This can mean that they are regularly forced to go along with things they don't agree with rather than feeling secure enough to state their own thoughts and ideas. They may not even be able to recognize when they're allowing themselves to be taken advantage of. They may find themselves regularly exhausted and exasperated by their overbearing friends but feel unable to stop negative cycles.

People who have come from homes that were abusive, neglectful, or unstable are likely, on some level, to connect feelings of love and attachment with *fear*. For instance, if your mother was narcissistic and dismissive of you, you may have grown up feeling afraid that she would reject you no matter what you did. You may have been scared of losing a parent's affection when they became abusive toward you due to their own emotional instability or when they were drunk.

You may have a deep rooted fear of abandonment that you have taken with you into your adult relationships; a *habit* of staying in relationships that are similar to the one you had with your primary caregiver. This relationship pattern could be causing things in your life to be unnecessarily hard, not to mention the damaging effects it may have on your self-esteem.

Perhaps you steer clear of telling your boss when you're unhappy with things at work because you're afraid they'll disagree or fire you. You might keep your mouth shut when your friends say things that hurt your feelings because you're afraid of conflict or rejection. You might allow your lover or partner to make all the decisions in your relationship or treat you poorly because deep down you're afraid they'll leave you if you speak up. Often these thoughts and feelings - these *patterns* - live deep in our subconscious. They control our every move without us even realizing it. But if you think about it for a while you might see how fear is tied to some or all of your attachment relationships. After much reflection you might see a correlation between your childhood relationships and those in your adulthood.

If you were raised without boundaries or positive attention, or if you were given too much responsibility as a child, you might be able to recognize that your current relationships are also lacking boundaries. You may struggle with authority or seek approval endlessly. You might often find yourself getting involved in friendships and intimate relationships wherein you act as caretaker. You might regularly put yourself in a parental or authoritative role when living or working with others; thus distancing and isolating yourself. You may get mistreated or feel disrespected and undervalued a lot. You may struggle with conflict resolution causing you to get hurt easily and allow your relationships to end suddenly or prematurely rather than attempt to overcome these challenges.

It goes without saying that tumultuous relationships can take a serious toll on your self esteem, whether you relationship troubles have developed as a result of a difficult childhood or they spring from a particularly painful time in your adulthood. But changing your relationship patterns and learning how to recognize when your relationships with others are lacking healthy boundaries is possible no matter what your background. By taking the time to think deeply about your needs and desires, and by practicing expressing yourself to others, you can have healthy, lasting relationships. Practice doing these things with someone you feel that you can trust.

Confide in them about your desire to have healthier relationships and ask them if they will encourage you to be more assertive with your thoughts and feelings. If you're used to going along with what other people say and do, practice saying "no" when you disagree with something. Try to express what you want to do or how you feel about the topic at hand without being swayed or intimidated by others. These things do take practice - unfortunately, these aren't things about ourselves that we can change overnight - but the more experience you have with setting boundaries, the easier it will become.

Being assertive is hard for everyone at one point or another but we all have the power and the *right* to have our needs heard. In order to ensure equality in your relationships, you have to learn how to put yourself first. You deserve to have a voice. You deserve to be able to express yourself without fear of ridicule or abandonment. During this time if you have certain friends or relatives that you believe will respond negatively to your assertiveness, don't start out by testing the waters with these people. Start experimenting with boundaries with people that are open, encouraging, and respectful toward you.

By doing these things every day you will find that you have more courage when it comes to speaking your mind in the future. Your relationships with others will be healthier and your self esteem will benefit dramatically.

Exercise #7

Take some time to think about how boundaries function in your relationships. Think about your family members, friends, work colleagues, and lovers.

Do you feel as though your relationships are lacking boundaries? Do you have a hard time being assertive about your needs, opinions, and desires?

Do you feel like your relationships are mutually beneficial or do you often feel drained by the people in your life?
Do you feel as though you get enough respect within your relationships?

Now think about what your relationships are lacking. Think about ways you could feel more emotionally safe or more respected. Think about ways that your relationships could be more equal.

Write down as many ideas as possible. Really let your mind open up and write down anything that you'd like to change.

For instance, do you feel as though your friends put too much pressure on you?
Do you feel like you support them but they don't support you?
Do you dislike the way someone in your life speaks to you?
Is there someone in your life that sends you a lot of mixed signals?
Is there someone that makes you feel inferior?
Do people in your life take advantage of you?
If you were sick or in trouble who would you call? Who wouldn't you call? Why?

Once you've written your list think about how you can create boundaries that will make your relationships safe and enjoyable.

For instance: If there are people in your life that regularly dismiss your emotions around difficult situations, can you be assertive about your needs?

If someone is disrespectful toward you, can you approach them about it? If not, a helpful boundary in this situation might be to refrain from talking to them about things they won't understand.

Is there someone who demands a lot of your time and energy? If you have a hard time saying "no" to them, consider talking to them about this issue. Allow yourself to say "no" if you need time for yourself. Remind yourself that you deserve to reserve some time and energy for you!

Putting boundaries in place is a way you can prioritize your needs and keep your relationships enjoyable and mutually beneficial.

Focus On the Right Areas To Improve Your Esteem

Quite often, people with low self-esteem fall into the role of caretaker in their relationships. This is because a lot of these people are extremely generous towards others and, as you read above, they can be endlessly compromising. Despite their habits of treating themselves poorly, people with low self-esteem are often known for how openly they express empathy, how warm they are towards others, and how understanding and sympathetic they can be with other people's feelings. People with low self-esteem that fall into this category tend to be fiercely loyal friends and lovers who often go above and beyond when it comes to care and concern for others. They celebrate the achievements of their friends sincerely and tend to be great listeners.

The problem arises when someone is so abundantly self*less* that they have an inability or a reluctance to treat themselves with the same care, attention, and compassion they do with others. These people are likely to struggle to accept kindness and generosity from others as well. Often, people with low self-esteem focus all their positivity on other people and reserve little to none for themselves. By the same rite they tend to reserve all their negative views, their criticisms and harsh judgments, for themselves.

This is another way that people with low self-esteem succeed in subconsciously putting themselves at the bottom of their list of priorities. If you're not giving yourself the same praise and positivity you offer your friends, you are activating telling yourself that you're not worthy, thus feeding your negative self beliefs. By constantly placing others above you, you are quietly telling yourself that you are inferior and less important than they are.

In addition, being just that little bit too selfless could lead you to enter relationships wherein you are taken advantage of or taken for granted. Although there is absolutely nothing wrong with being a generous and understanding person, it's important to question why you find it so much easier to care for others than you do for yourself.

Ask yourself:

*Are you continuously doling out your love, kindness, and care out to other people but starving yourself of the same thing?

*If you're the type of person who spends all their positive energy on others, how much of that beneficial energy could you possibly have left for yourself?

*Are you focusing all of your energy on other people to avoid focusing on yourself?

*Are you focusing on other people's needs as a way to avoid recognizing your own? If so, why?

*Do you believe you are not worthy of the compassion you offer to other people?

*Do you regularly downsize your accomplishments or minimize your struggles in the face of others?

*What would it feel like to care for yourself the way you care for other people?

No matter who you are or where you're from you deserve kindness, warmth, and understanding. You deserve to be proud of your accomplishments, big or small! Deep down you probably know this as you are already taking measures to ditch your bad habits and be kinder to yourself. It's important to note that though you may often seek approval and respect from others, the most important person you need this warmth and positivity from is you.

You need to be able to tell yourself that you're worthy of being cared for. In order to be able to accept love from someone else, you must first learn how to accept it from yourself. In order to be respected by another person, you must first learn to respect yourself. Being selfless can be a beautiful quality, but if it means starving yourself of pride, care, solace, or love, it's not worth it.

Every human being needs and deserves love. Until you can show yourself respect and kindness you will never truly be able to accept it from others. This could mean alienating yourself, missing out on career opportunities, or letting romantic love pass you by. If you have a pattern of being in relationships wherein you play the role of 'caretaker' think about why this is. Take a minute to imagine yourself in a relationship or friendship where both parties are equal.

Both parties have ups and downs, both have high moments and low moments. Both parties give and take, both respect and value one another. Most importantly, both parties accept and love themselves as individuals and they aren't afraid of expressing their needs to one another. If the idea of a relationship like this makes you uncomfortable, take some time to think about why that is. If you regularly place all your worry and care on other people or you feel as though you have to be strong for them, ask yourself why.

Are you afraid to be weak or vulnerable with others? If so, why? If you spend a lot of your time and energy on helping others through their problems, is it possible that this is just a way for you to avoid your own? Are you diminishing the importance of your problems for the sake of other people? Do you ever ask for help?

Remember, attachment relationships should be equal and respectful. You can spend as much positive energy on other people as you like, but you don't have to sacrifice yourself, your feelings, or your beliefs in the meantime. Try to offer yourself the same positivity you offer to others, rather than putting yourself down. Reserve some energy for yourself. And be mindful of when you start to slip into bad habits.

Another note worth mentioning in this section is that some selfless people often don't like to *complain*. They feel that their complaints about life impose on other people or affect them negatively, even when their "complaints" are actually valid concerns. It's important to remember that everyone experiences pain and suffering in life - to many degrees - and everyone needs a chance to get things off their chest from time to time. We all go through difficult times in life. We all experience negativity and hardship.

Being able to rely on our friends and loved ones to help us get through these times is extremely important for our emotional wellbeing. Sometimes in life we have to put on a brave face, but we can't possibly keep that mask on at all times. Trapping our thoughts and feelings inside us rarely turns out well; it certainly doesn't make them any easier to cope with.

It's fair to say that complaining *all* the time is usually unproductive but there's nothing wrong with leaning on your loved ones in times of need. Many times in our lives we really do need other people. We need their opinions to help us make decisions and we need to feel like we're not alone in this world. Don't forget, human beings are born into *groups*.

This is because we are happier, more productive, and have a better sense of security when in the company of others than we would if we were completely isolated. We all benefit from having other people to help us through our feelings and difficult experiences. We need the support and compassion of others.

Some selfless individuals focus spend so much of their time and energy on other people's difficulties that they downsize their own and refuse to give it the attention it requires. They tell themselves that they have "nothing to complain about" or that they'd rather not bother their friends with their problems. You might believe that other people have suffered more than you - and you're probably right to some degree - but that doesn't make your pain any less valid. It's not inappropriate to sound off about things that are troubling you in the presence of your loved ones. There is no reason why you should deserve any less when it comes to empathy, kindness, and support.

In order for you to learn how to love yourself it's vital that you treat yourself with the same care and attention that you would offer a friend. Offering yourself regular acts of self-care and practicing positive self-talk is an extremely important part of your journey to healthy self-esteem. These daily practices may seem insignificant; you might think that there's no way such subtle changes can really make a difference in your life. But I promise you that doing these little things every day is crucial when it comes to sending the right messages to yourself. In order to start really loving yourself, be persistent about letting go of your bad habits and implementing good

I struggle with this↓

ones. Start treating yourself nicely when you're having a tough time rather than putting yourself down or belittling your problems.

When you are in an emotionally safe situation, challenge yourself open up to your friends and loved ones. If you're not used to doing this, learning to trust other people and share your struggles with them will be hard at first. You may find it difficult to accept sympathy and compassion from others. However, remember that love and affection are part of our basic human needs, as is feeling as though we belong to a community. These are things we all need and deserve.

A big part of good to yourself means *listening* to yourself when you're not feeling the best. Really let yourself hear your thoughts and feelings rather than trying to ignore or minimize them. If you're feeling upset about something, try to recognize the truth in that. Instead of saying, "at least I don't have it as bad as so-and-so", allow yourself to experience your true feelings.

Remember, your feelings just want to be felt and your thoughts want to be heard. Although negative feelings can be challenging, they will leave you far more quickly if you give them the attention they require. You don't have to wallow in your problems or let them overcome you. Just listen to them, give them your attention, and let them go. If they return, do the same again.

Go easy on yourself, be kind to yourself. Try to express yourself to someone who can offer you support whenever possible. This will be challenging if you're not used to sharing your problems with others but you will benefit greatly from doing so. Feelings of sadness, anger, and frustration do not have to be a burden. They don't have to overwhelm you. But if allow yourself to ignore your thoughts and feelings, they're much more likely to eat away at you and become bigger than you can handle. It's vital that you learn how to start listening to yourself and treating yourself nicely in order to diminish the effect negative emotions have on you.

Whatever emotion or situation you are confronted with, imagine a friend were in the same predicament like you did in *Exercise #2*.

Think about what you would say or do to support your friend and help them through this difficult time. Then practice doing the same for yourself. I use the word 'practice' a lot in this book but these things really do take practice! If you are used to beating yourself up or disallowing yourself positive attention or self-care, it will take some time and effort to undo those patterns.

Self-soothing is a skill and it might take time to learn how to do it if you're not used to caring for yourself. If you feel like you're being selfish by treating yourself kindly and making time for yourself, you must learn to let that go. There is a *big* and very important difference between taking good care of yourself and being selfish.

What do they always say during safety briefs on airlines? "Take care of your own oxygen mask before helping others".

It's okay to say **"no"** to your friends from time to time if you don't have the energy to help them. Making yourself a priority does not mean that you care less about anyone else in your life. It is not something to feel guilty about. Remind yourself often that your needs and desires matter just as much as everyone else's! More than anything, remember that this is *your* life. It's up to you to make it what you want it to be. Don't let it slip through your fingers.

We are only on this earth for a short time. If you have struggled a lot in life, tell yourself that it's time to let go. You have struggled enough. You have the power to make the rest of your life enjoyable, light, fun, and full of warmth and excitement. You hold all the cards.

Self-Esteem and Romantic Relationships

For people struggling with low self-esteem, managing and maintaining romantic relationships can be extremely difficult. Relationships can be challenging for everyone at one time or another. Making sure that both parties' needs are met, that both people feel physically and emotionally safe in the relationship, and that both are respectful and supportive of each other isn't always easy. Loving relationships need work sometimes and they demand our attention.

They must be fed with compromise, understanding, and mutually beneficial constructs. Romantic relationships can be wonderful when things go well but if your relationship history is a little rough around the edges, the idea of romance might terrify you. And if you don't feel great about yourself, it can be especially hard to let another person love you.

If you have a habit of putting yourself last, you might allow yourself to be treated poorly or taken advantage of. If your childhood was full of dysfunctional relationships, your relationship pattern might need some tweaking. If you have issues with control and/or a habit of being the caretaker in your relationships, you may act more like a parent to your partner than a lover. If you have had a few romantic partners in your life but none of them lasted, it's time to start thinking about why. Your unsuccessful relationship history could be a major player in your current self-beliefs and your behavior towards other people.

For instance, you may be focusing on your past mistakes and using them as an excuse to stay away from romance or to keep people at arm's length rather than allowing yourself to get involved with love again. You might be in the habit of completely isolating yourself from others.

You might self-sabotage or have a tendency to *'quit while you're ahead'* when relationships are going well. Similarly, if your past relationships involved having someone criticize you or judge you harshly (including relationships with your family members or friends), you may be reluctant to jump into another relationship in a hurry. But it's important to remind yourself again and again: The fact that things have ended badly in the past does not mean that they are bound to do the same again. You have the power to change the course of your life.

By rebuilding your self-esteem and thinking about what you really want and need from another person, you can change your relationship pattern and turn it into something positive. The same is true if you are in a relationship now that you feel could benefit from a little TLC. Taking some time to evaluate your relationships and how they make you feel is beneficial to everyone.

Getting into a romantic relationship can be exciting, intimate, tender, and passionate, but for some people it can also be frightening or even panic inducing. If you're afraid of getting into a relationship, or you actively keep yourself away from romantic opportunities, think about why.

Ask yourself:
*Do you believe that you aren't 'good enough' or that you don't deserve love?
*Are you afraid that you will repeat past mistakes; that you will hurt someone or be hurt by someone?
*Do you believe that you can't possibly be right for someone else or that no one would want to be with you?
*Do you think you are unloveable or incapable of loving someone else?
*Are your poor self-beliefs dictating your potential for healthy, loving relationships?
*Do you blame yourself for the ending of past relationships?
*Do you believe that you can't be in a relationship because you're 'different' than other people?
*Do you believe that if you let someone get close to you, you'll let them down in the future?
*Are you using negative thoughts about yourself and your past as an excuse to avoid entering relationships in the present?

Relationships can be complicated but having a difficult relationship past doesn't mean you're bound to have a difficult relationship future. Healthy relationships are mutually beneficial, they meet the needs of both individuals simultaneously. They are based on respect, honesty, and trust. They demand us to love another person while allowing that person to love us in return. It can be extremely difficult for people with low self-esteem to believe that they are worthy of love and affection and this can cause serious problems in relationships.

For instance, if you feel that you are not worthy of your partner, your behavior towards them can become toxic. You may become jealous, needy, or untrusting; constantly devaluing yourself, pushing your partner away, or clinging to them for dear life. It is unfortunate how closely knit low self-esteem and jealousy can be. If you're feeling insecure, unloveable, or threatened by other people, jealousy usually isn't far away. This can create serious trust issues between you and your partner. Jealousy can make people act in extreme ways. It can cause people to act suspicious, to lie or deceive, to become stiflingly close to one another, or to head for the hills. It's not hard to imagine how difficult it can be to keep jealousy at bay when your self-esteem is plummeting.

The trust you feel for your partner isn't just based on how you feel about them. It is also very closely linked to how you feel about yourself. If you're feeling insecure or under par, it's easy to feel threatened by other people in your partners' life. You may feel nervous when they go out with their friends for the night or you may become suspicious of one someone your partner works with who you feel threatened by. If these scenarios sound familiar, take some time to think about why.

Are these valid concerns? i.e. has your partner cheated or lied to you before?
Have they expressed an interest in someone else?
Or are these negative thoughts directly related to how you feel about yourself?
Are your poor self-beliefs making you expect the worst?

Whether your instinct is to hold tight to your partner or you're more likely to disallow others from getting close to you in the first place, it's important to think about how self-esteem, fear, and jealousy function in your romantic relationships.

It's necessary to note the importance of individuality and privacy within romantic relationships. As previously discussed regarding your relationship with your primary caregiver, we all need a sense of autonomy, a sense of ourselves outside the confines of anyone else. If you lacked autonomy as a child, you are likely to experience adult relationships where the same is true. You may be *'clingy'* by nature. You and your partner may become more of a duo rather than two individuals in a loving relationship; more like conjoined twins than two people who have chosen to be in a room together. If you and your partner are always together (or always in touch), this could be because you're afraid of being apart. Without having your partner closely connected to you at all times, you may experience anxiety, surges of jealousy, or feelings of abandonment and impending doom.

Ask yourself now: Do you feel emotionally fragile when you and your partner part ways? Do you experience anxiety, jealousy, or sadness when your partner calls you less frequently or sends you fewer texts than usual?

Let's say that the two of you spend every waking minute together but one of you has to go away for the weekend. Without a strong sense of self you might feel listless without your partner. You might feel agitated, suspicious, nervous, or exceedingly lonely. If this is how you feel about spending a weekend apart, how would you feel if the relationship ended for good? For people with low self-esteem, attachment relationships can be so intense that when they end you're left in an extremely fragile and emotionally dangerous state. You may feel buried beneath feelings of rejection and longing. Even if you were the person who ended the relationship, you could still experience an onslaught of depression and increasingly negative self-beliefs.

Understanding what emotions are at work in situations like these is important when it comes to making a change in your relationship pattern. Spend some time reflecting on these ideas now. Think about how your self-esteem factors into your behavior within romantic relationships. If you are needy or highly sensitive in relationships, think about how setting healthy boundaries could help protect you from emotional pain in the future. Human beings need to feel self-reliant and each of us needs privacy.

If you find yourself getting jealous or fearful when your partner carves out some alone time, ask yourself what's really behind those feelings?
Are you afraid that your partner will leave or betray you?
Do you believe that their desire to be alone is directly related to how they feel about you?
Is it possible that they simply value their autonomy within the relationship?
If you feel threatened by this behavior, do you feel that way because of something *they* did or something that happened to *you* in the past with someone else?

Think about how much alone time you have within your relationship as well. It's important for us to have quiet time, to be alone with our thoughts or engage in activities we enjoy. Whether you're in a relationship or not, you need autonomy. You need a sense of your life belonging to you. Having your own friends or activities you enjoy outside your romantic relationship is necessary for building and maintaining a strong sense of self as well as nurturing the trust you and your partner have for one another.

Along similar lines, if your relationship with your primary caregiver was particularly fragile; that is, if they constantly sent you mixed signals, made you feel insignificant or unremarkable, or made you 'chase' them for their love; you are likely to pair up with people who treat you the same way in adulthood. For instance, if your mother was neglectful, you may have spent your childhood constantly trying to impress her or win her approval. All of your actions may have been subconsciously designed to secure her love and attention. But if you spent your whole childhood in that type of cyclical, damaging relationship where you were never good enough, it's likely that you have entered adult relationships that are similar in one way or another.

Perhaps you chase people who won't get into a real relationship with you; people who are elusive with their love, who send you mixed signals and never quite give you what you want from them. You're more likely to long for lovers who never accept your love or who don't like you get too close to them rather than choosing to be with someone who openly loves and respects you. When it comes to relationships blueprints and patterns it's pretty clear to see how your past functions in your present if this is the case in your love life.

What does it look like when you are in a romantic relationship?
Are you often unsure how your partner really feels about you?
Do you think that they're tuned in to your feelings?
Do they respond to your thoughts and feelings with respect and care?
Do you live to impress them?

Maybe you do things for the sole purpose of gaining their approval. Perhaps you feel devastated if they don't notice or mention your achievements.

It's important to tell yourself that you should not have to chase anyone for their love. No one should. In a relationship where this is the case, you're likely to feel endlessly inferior. You may feel fragile or fearful, constantly holding your breath waiting for the relationships to spontaneously end. Or you're likely to become heartbroken when your partners' approval is not met. Feeling like your relationship could end at any moment is exhausting and stressful, but if you're not used to being with someone who expresses love and respect freely, you might continue getting into damaging relationships like this based on instinct alone. The decision to get into relationships like this is hardly ever a conscious one. All of us subconsciously repeat the relationships blueprint laid out for us by our primary caregivers to some degree and it takes practice to break out of those molds.

You must remember the importance of individuality for both you and your partner. Being able to be your true self, to follow your own path and respect yourself, is extremely important to your feelings of self worth and to your overall happiness. Allowing yourself to be with someone who loves and respects you outwardly can feel alien to someone who's used to chasing love but if you recognize this pattern in yourself, it's time to start making some changes.

One thing that can be extremely hard for people with low self-esteem is the idea that someone has chosen to be with you. You might feel like you're not worthy of love, you might not trust yourself, or you might not even understand why someone else would want to be with you. In fact, you may be the one in the relationship who is elusive with affection. You might be the one keeping your partner at arm's length and sending mixed signals. What role you play is based on your relationship blueprint and it's important to note that not all people with low self-esteem will behave exactly the same when it comes to relationships! The important thing is to understand that allowing yourself to love and be loved is a common struggle for people with low self-esteem. It can take a lot to battle feelings of being 'not good enough' or 'incapable of successful relationships'.

Remind yourself that if someone wants to spend their time with you - even if you can't understand why that is - you have to accept that being with you is *their* choice. If they didn't want to be with you they wouldn't have chosen you. You have to learn to accept it when your partner offers their love to you, not question or negate it. Don't try to convince someone else that you're not worthy of them. Trust that they chose you because you *are* worthy of them. Relationships will always have ups and downs, people will always make mistakes, but living in fear will not serve you when it comes to love. Keeping yourself away from romantic relationships could be a way of punishing yourself; depriving yourself of the love and affection you need and deserve. Try not to overthink things. Ease up a bit and try to let yourself just go with the flow.

At the end of the day, relationships are meant to bring us companionship and joy, not fear and negativity.

In the last two sections you learned about what self-esteem is, how it functions in our lives, and some ways yours may have been shaped by events in your life. I touched upon childhood and how our early relationships affect us, how being overly selfless can cause you to put yourself last on your list of priorities, and how low self esteem functions in romantic relationships. In part three, I will focus on ways you can start to feel better about yourself and get more out of life. I will talk about ways you can rewire your thinking and challenge your relationship blueprint. I will touch upon the importance of setting realistic goals and judging yourself by your own criteria. This section will also cover some practical things you can do to boost your self-esteem and brighten your days.

Getting More Out of Life

When your self esteem isn't at its best, it's common to rerun negative thoughts and experiences in your mind over and over again. When you're feeling low, it's almost as if your negative past experiences come back to haunt you, kicking you when you're down. You might indulge in reruns of embarrassing moments, times you said or did things you wish you hadn't have. You might fall into the hands of negative self-talk, telling yourself that you're stupid, weird, or awkward; that you don't matter, you're not good enough, or that you're inferior to other people. It's strange how when we're not feeling good about ourselves, we immerse ourselves in negative thoughts and memories that can hurt us.

When we're low it can be almost impossible to think of ourselves in a positive light at all. Rather in these times, when we are most in need of positivity and kindness, we allow ourselves to get swept away in a tide of self-loathing and negativity. Learning how to quiet those voices from the past takes practice and dedication. Being mindful of your feelings and treating yourself with care can be difficult if you're used to treating yourself poorly. This is another point where indulging in regular self care and practicing positive self-talk is particularly helpful.

Dedicating yourself to doing nice things just for you every day works incredibly well when it comes to gradually chipping away your negative self-beliefs. It's a subtle way of sending positive messages to your self-esteem. And the more you do it, the more you will feel the benefit of it. Eventually, doing nice things for yourself will become second nature and you'll notice a rise in both your mood and your self-esteem. So too, remembering to treat yourself like a friend when times are tough is vital to keeping your self-esteem out of the gutter. If your friend was feeling low, would you remind them of every time in their past when they made a mistake or did something embarrassing? Of course you wouldn't! Listening to your thoughts and recognizing when they're going down an unhelpful or harmful path is extremely important. When you notice yourself doing this, make a resolve to stop it immediately.

Say to yourself what you would say to a friend. Don't let your mind drag you down a path of self-hatred. Instead, stop the negative thoughts in their tracks and try to turn them around. Think about the things you have achieved, not the things you haven't achieved or the things you could've done better. Do something nice for yourself. Treat yourself with love and understanding. Forgive yourself for your mistakes and move on.

If you have felt 'different' throughout your life you may have developed a belief system that continues to set your apart from others in adulthood. This may include negative expectations of how your life is bound to turn out, strong beliefs about things you can't have or will never be able to do in life. You might make sweeping statements about the things in life that you deem to be impossible for you. If you have low expectations for yourself and your future, it's likely that those beliefs spring from feeling undervalued or overlooked in your childhood and/or early adulthood. Wounds like this can take time to fully heal. Recovering from painful events in our past takes time and patience but it's important to do what you can to start rooting your thoughts in the here and now. Let go of the things you can't change and focus on the things you can. Stop focusing on external factors and start focusing on you.

Self-doubt can be hard to conquer, especially if it's something you've had for most of your life. Believing in yourself isn't easy if you've never done it before! If you have a habit of judging yourself harshly, putting yourself down, or making constant negative assessments of yourself and your achievements, it's no wonder your self beliefs are so poor! The problem with self-doubt is that it can live within you like a seed planted in your gut.

Each time you fail to accomplish something, each time you experience rejection or embarrassment, that seed gets watered. If you've ever tried to pull a thick stemmed weed out of concrete and found it nearly impossible to do, think of self-doubt in the same light. It has strong, ruthless roots and it clings the space it occupies within you, often strangling your self-confidence in the meantime.

The only way to get rid of it is to kill it all the way down to its roots. Otherwise you might resign yourself to a life that's lacking in love, excitement, achievement, pride, or happiness. You may develop tendencies to overwork yourself, keep romantic relationships brief and/or lacking in depth, and deny yourself the good things in life. Everyone experiences fleeting moments of self doubt and that is completely normal; however, if you have been plagued with it for most of your life, you'll need to develop some strength when it comes to obliterating it.

If you're accustomed to viewing yourself as *'different'* from other people and you've convinced yourself that you cannot or should not have what other people have, it's time to start rewiring your thinking. Human beings are complex. We all suffer. We all have dark moments. We all experience hardship, grief, and sacrifice. One of the most incredible things about human beings is that we are tied together by how different we each are. In a way, it is our *difference* that makes us the same. No other person has had the life you've had. There has never been a single other person with your physiological and psychological make up. But you can be sure that no matter what you're feeling at any given moment, someone else has felt the same way. We are, each of us, different. And strikingly, that's the one thing that we all have in common: our autonomy, our individuality, the things that make us each special.

No matter who you are or where you come from, there is no reason why you should deserve less than other people. No two people are the same. Being different is being human. Being *different* is being the *same*. Your life can be just as fulfilling, satisfying, and enjoyable as anyone else's. Practice leaving whatever happened in the past behind you. The present and future are yours for the taking. Tell yourself regularly that you are worthy of having the life you want.

A common hurdle that people with low self-esteem have to overcome is understanding the value system with which they judge themselves. In life, if we are to truly love ourselves, we must judge ourselves by our own criteria. This means trusting in yourself and your own value system rather than comparing yourself to other people or trying to live up to social ideals that don't interest you. This can be hard to do as we live in a time when we are surrounded with advertisements about what our lives *should* be like. We are subject to an onslaught of other people's daily lives on social media. But what you see online or on TV often isn't the whole truth.

Mostly, the stuff people put online is the stuff they want people to see. They project images of themselves that make them look the way they want people to perceive them and it's important to keep perspective about this if you spend a lot of time online. The Internet can make it pretty easy to get caught in a trap of negative self evaluation. But trying to live up to ideals that you may not even believe in is a waste of your time and energy. Think hard about the values that you possess as an individual and try to base your self-assessments on these things rather than what the world around you is encouraging you to do.

What is important to *you*?
Is money an important factor in your life?
Power? Love? Material possessions?
Being a good parent? Being a good citizen?
Having friends?

Contributing to society?
Having time to spend on hobbies and recreation?
Following your dreams?
Having a successful career?

Whatever is important to you is what matters in your life. Thinking along these lines is a much more realistic and fair way to assess yourself and your accomplishments. Once you're willing to judge yourself based on your own criteria you can make plans and take steps to achieve your personal goals. There is no point in beating yourself about things you haven't achieved if you never really wanted them in the first place!

Comparing yourself to other people can be unhealthy and dangerous. It can make you feel ostracized, isolated, and less important than other people. Yet so many of us do it day in and day out. It can be hard not to! We go online and punish ourselves for not being like other people or for not having the things they have. Online, everyone's life looks better than ours. Everyone else seems to possess the qualities we want for ourselves. The thing is, using other people as a template of what you and your life *should* be like is a habit that can easily backfire. We can easily turn other people's accomplishments into weapons to hurt ourselves with. Hence, comparing ourselves to other people is a behavior that needs to be stamped out.

When you assess your life by comparing yourself to others, you're likely to skim over some important details. No one knows the ins and outs of another person's life completely. No one knows the private pains that other people experience nor the personal challenges they face on a daily basis. Rather, when we compare ourselves to other people, we usually pick and choose what we want use against ourselves, what we *think* we know about them. We see our neighbors looking like the perfect family - a house, two kids, a nice car, regular vacations - and make assessments about them based on these surface facts. We beat ourselves up for how unlike them we are, how little we have compared to them.

We make judgments about ourselves that actively set us apart from them; things that make us look like fungus growing in the shadow of their giant oak tree. But when we do this we are purposely hurting ourselves, telling ourselves that we're not good enough. And ironically, underneath it all we have no idea if the way we perceive other people is even accurate! We indulge in this comparison for the sole purpose of making ourselves feel worthless. Rather than being realistic about our own lives, we choose to look at other people's lives, focusing on the things that make us feel jealous, resentful, or bitter.

In order to stop comparing ourselves from others we must first stop setting ourselves apart from them. Of course you are *different* from other people, the same way that everybody is different from everybody else. Using the idea of *difference* to keep you from loving yourself or to prevent you from reaching your own personal goals is unhelpful and unnecessarily harmful to your self-esteem. The more times you say things like *"I can't be in a relationship because I'm different from other people"*, *"other people have it so much easier than me"*, *"I'll never have the type of life other people have"*, or *"I just wasn't meant to live like other people"*, the more you'll begin to believe what you're saying.

If you tell yourself that you aren't capable of having enjoyable relationships or satisfying life experiences because you're not like other people, you're setting yourself up for a lifetime of failure and self-pity. You're sending a message to yourself that will only hold you back in life.

Indulging in negative mantras like these is actually quite interesting because there is something about doing this that gives us permission to give up on ourselves. It's almost like by expecting the worst for yourself, you won't be too disappointed if you don't achieve what you'd hoped for. But repeating these things to yourself does not minimize disappointment by any stretch of the imagination. It does the exact opposite. Repeating negative prophecies for yourself means eventually you'll simply stop trying - stop *hoping* - for more.

Each of us have tried and failed before, some of us many times over. Failure can be hard to recover from but allowing yourself to be defeated by it, or taking immense amounts of self-doubt from it will not serve you. Repeating these negative mantras is actively telling yourself that you don't believe in yourself. You would never do that to a friend so why do it to yourself? Comparing yourself to other people and indulging in negative self talk are both harmful habits that need to be stopped.

Try to recognize when you think or say phrases that are laden with self-doubt. When you notice yourself comparing yourself to others - aloud or in your head - tell yourself to **STOP**. When you hear yourself saying things like *"I should have [...] by now"* or *"there's no way I'll ever achieve [..]"* recognize the thought, challenge it, and put a stop to it. Then try to turn it around.

Ask yourself:

*Have I done this to the best of my ability?
*Is there anything more I can do to work towards this goal?
*Is there any real reason I can't achieve what I want?
*Am I holding myself back from trying something because I'm scared of failure?
*Can I survive failure? Have I survived it before?
*Am I getting all I want out of life or am I preventing myself from going after the things I really want?
*Why do I think other people are worthy of things that I disallow myself?
*Are my feelings of self doubt rooted in truth, fear, or habit?
*Is there any real reason why I shouldn't give myself another shot?
*Am I happy the way things are or is it time for a change?

When negative thoughts arise, tell yourself that if you can't say something nice, don't say anything at all. Repeating negative mantras will only hurt you. Set yourself free from them. Believe in yourself. You deserve the same opportunities as everyone else in this world. You are worthy and capable of having positive relationships, career success, and the same comforts and luxuries as everyone else.

You may very well be different than other people, but being different does not make you worthless nor incapable.

You may have had a rough start in life but you're capable of healing from that and having the life you want. Get more out of life by simply allowing yourself to have more. Allow yourself to have desires. Allow yourself to be loved. Allow yourself to have opportunities and luxuries. Allow yourself to take risks. Allow yourself to go for what you really want in life. And if you fail, so what? Go easy on yourself and allow yourself to try again!

Exercise #8

In order to start holding yourself in higher esteem, it is imperative that you learn to stop negative thoughts from running your life and ruining your self-image. Retraining your thoughts isn't easy. If you've developed a habit of judging yourself harshly, it will take some time to break it. The next time you hear yourself focusing on what you didn't do or what you could've done better, challenge yourself to stop the thought and turn it around. Focus on what you *did* accomplish instead.

For example, if you hear yourself saying:
"I joined the gym but I've only gone once or twice. I'm not very fit. I only worked out for twenty minutes and I was completely out of breath. I was mortified."

Recognize the negativity in those thoughts and **STOP** it. Turn it around and refocus on the positive.

Say:
"Joining the gym was a fear of mine and I faced it! I had made a lot of excuses in the past to avoid exercising in front of other people and it was pretty tough, but I'm sure it will get easier and I'm proud of myself for finally going."

If you're used to putting yourself down, learning to go easy on yourself will take practice. Start by trying to recognize negative thoughts when they first strike. If you struggle to turn the thought around completely, do your best to at least stop it in its tracks. Ask a friend or loved one to help you with this. Have them listen out for any times you say negative things about yourself and encourage you to turn it around. These things may feel silly at the start but with repetition, they really do work!

Your Self-Esteem and Dealing With The People Around You

Your self-esteem is a precious and fragile thing that lies deep inside you, but unfortunately you're not the only one who gets to handle it. Throughout your life many people will have a chance to put their stamp on your self worth. I have often said that sharing the earth with other human beings can simultaneously be the most comforting and the most challenging part of life. Without other people to share our lives with, the world would be a terrible place. We take great comfort in other people. We celebrate together, we laugh together, we rely on one another. But when another person is hurtful towards us, when they are careless with our emotions or when they act as our enemy, our self-esteem can really take a hit.

For those of us who are particularly sensitive, relationships with other human beings can cause an astounding amount of anxiety and pain. Enduring disapproval or rejection can really take its toll. If you grew up in a family wherein you were commonly treated as the scapegoat; that is to say, it seemed like everything was your fault and you couldn't do anything right; you may have grown up to be particularly fragile when it comes to receiving criticism from others. You might find it hard to understand how other people can be so resilient in the face of adversity while you find it extremely challenging.

It's important to remember that everyone has their own threshold when it comes to things like this. When people say or do hurtful things to each other, one person may merely shrug it off and forget about it immediately while another might take it to heart and experience long lasting negative emotions because of it. We are all different in this way. Becoming resilient, or developing a 'thick skin' isn't easy but there are ways you can reduce the force at which you experience criticism.

When you feel hurt or ridiculed by another person, remind yourself of your personal value system. Think about your values and your standards and judge yourself accordingly. Ask yourself why the criticism you received hurt as much as it did.

Was it because it showcased a way in which you did not live up to your own standards? If so, forgive yourself and think about how you can move forward from here rather than beating yourself up over it and holding onto your negative feelings. Think about the function of your emotions.

What is that pang of embarrassment, shame, guilt, or rejection telling you?
What can you *do* with these emotions?
Can you turn them into something you can use?
Can you use them to learn something about yourself, your needs, or your goals?
Can you use this negative experience as a catalyst for something you'd like to change about yourself or something you'd like to be better at?

If you can turn the negatives into something positive, make a resolution to do so. Remember, when emotions are running high, go easy on yourself. Beating yourself up won't solve anything, it will only bring you further down.

If however, the negative feelings you develop after a conflict do not have a function beyond hurting you; that is to say, they can't be turned into anything positive; ask yourself why you're holding onto them.

Is this experience reminding you of something that happened in the past that is still unresolved?
Is it reminding you of how another person in your life once treated you or making you think about a past failure?
Is there anything you can *do* with these emotions?
Are there any conflicts that can be resolved as a result?

If there is nothing you can change about the situation, nothing you can do to turn it around, it's probably best to gain perspective and let it go. Think about this situation in the grand scheme of life. Think about it in comparison with things you have experienced and overcome in the past. Ask yourself if focusing on this insult is serving you or if it's only bringing you down. Keep your own standards to mind and allow yourself to let it go. If you find yourself holding onto negative emotions, taking some quiet time for yourself, practicing meditation, or getting some physical exercise could be of great benefit to you.

Often, if we're used to experiencing negative emotions we hold onto them out of habit or familiarity, even when they're hurting us. If you have trouble releasing yourself from your racing negative thoughts, designate some time to think about them. Set a timer for ten to twenty minutes and let yourself try to make sense of the situation. Think about why you feel the way you do and seek to come to a conclusion. When the timer goes off, tell yourself to leave it behind you for the rest of the day. Once you have addressed and resolved the situation in your head don't let yourself return to it. Try to focus on other things, keep active, and practice extra self care until you feel better.

A lot of situations in our adult lives remind us of painful experiences from our pasts and these things can be particularly hard to endure. If you were rejected by an abusive or neglectful parent, you may struggle with feelings of rejection throughout your life. Whether you're going through a break up, you didn't get a job you applied for, or someone disagreed with an idea you had, it's okay to feel upset. For those people who experienced a lot of rejection in their childhoods, it's only natural to find coping with rejection difficult. But freeing yourself from these particular fears, anxieties, and heartbreaks is possible, and you don't have to keep others at arm's length in order to do so! Think of your past experiences with rejection as just a little extra challenge in your life, nothing more than that. You may react sensitively to rejection throughout your life but recognizing that it's something you struggle with is the first step to overcoming it. There is nothing wrong with being sensitive. It is not something to beat yourself up over.

Be strong in yourself. Love yourself. Your painful past does not have to maintain its hold on you forever. If you have a habit of being cruel to yourself or believing that you're not good enough, in a way what you're actually doing *rejecting yourself* and that's something no one needs in the face of adversity! By learning to accept yourself for who you are - by learning to *love* yourself - your self confidence and self esteem will eventually be strong enough to withstand the insensitivities of others.

Practice asking yourself what it is about rejection that bothers you so much.

What feelings does it evoke and where do they come from?
Do you only experience them when the rejection relates to your personal standards or is rejection something that can hurt no matter what the topic?

Think about what painful experiences in your past have contributed to your feelings in the present. In an effort to gain perspective, the next time you experience rejection, think about *detaching* the incident that's happening in your present from the experiences that happened in your past. Think of those experiences in your past like an anchor weighing you down. Visualize yourself cutting the tie between the past and present and let yourself focus on what's happening in the here and now. What's happening now is an isolated incident. It doesn't have to be a reminder of the past. Recognize how small it is when it's on its own. Chip away at it over time and eventually it will fade into nothing.

It's true that at times, people can be cruel and unnecessarily hurtful towards one another. They can be judgmental, deceptive, and ruthless with your feelings, and there's no denying that this can be an extremely frustrating and painful part of life. Coping with conflict isn't easy for the best of us, but when it comes to enduring the judgment of others, it's up to you to protect yourself. We cannot change other people's opinions about us, no matter how much we disagree with them or how much they hurt. We may seek to stand up for ourselves if we've been misunderstood or unfairly scorned but there is little we can do beyond that.

Sometimes it's hard to face the fact that not everyone in the world is going to like you. But it's important to realize that the same is true for everyone. You yourself will not like everyone in the world either! There are certain personality types that just don't mix well and there's nothing wrong with that. As I mentioned earlier regarding romantic love, be careful about chasing people in an effort to change their feelings about you. You might be punishing yourself unnecessarily by subconsciously reliving the relationship you had with your primary caregiver over and over again. Seek to spend your time with people who respect you and lift you up rather than chasing those who put you down. Start setting clear boundaries in your friendships and other relationships in an effort to keep yourself emotionally safe.

Trying to change other people's feelings about you is often a lost cause. Sometimes the best thing you can do is let other people's criticism roll off you like water off a duck's back. If you are being judged unnecessarily harshly, don't join the firing squad! Don't use other people's harsh words as an excuse to beat yourself up! Be a good friend to yourself. When it comes to people who are unfairly critical of you, try to tell yourself that their opinions are none of your business. What other people think about you is *their* business. Let them have their opinions. Focus on what you like about you. Focus on people who are good to you.

For people with low self-esteem learning how to trust yourself can be tricky. Trusting your instincts and your capabilities might feel foreign to you. Trusting your own *feelings* can present a hurdle, especially if you grew up having a parent negate or neglect them. If no one took you seriously growing up, it's more than possible that you'll have a hard time taking yourself seriously as an adult. But when it comes to resiliency and coping with rejection, trusting yourself can mean the difference between being devastated and simply being peeved. The key is in learning how to *approve* of yourself so that you're not reliant on the approval of others. This can be a long process but it's exactly what needs to happen if you really want to cope better with rejection, let go of your negative self-beliefs, and feel good about yourself. Keep your self-talk positive and beneficial and resist the urge to indulge in self-doubt or ridicule.

If you struggle with feelings of low self-worth it's common to seek the approval of others. It's almost as though your accomplishments are completely worthless if another person isn't there to witness them. Sort of like when a tree falls in the woods... does it make a sound if no one's there to hear it? When you do something positive; that is, when you accomplish something you've worked hard on or when you live up to your own standards; does that accomplishment cease to exist if no one's around to see it?

Ask yourself:
*Are you able to feel good about the things you accomplish?
*Do you allow yourself to feel *proud* of yourself, even if you're the only one who knows about it?
*Do you feel that you *can* approve of yourself? If so, is having that approval enough?
*How often do you approve of yourself or offer yourself rewards for your achievements?
If you rarely approve of yourself or if you feel like approving of yourself isn't enough, think about why this is.

Learning to accept your own approval and having that be enough is a powerful part of self-growth and I encourage you to think on this theme often. Being able recognize when you have achieved something which is praiseworthy is an important skill to have. Learning to approve of yourself will play a massive part in your journey towards overcoming your problems with low self-esteem. Feelings of self -approval do not always come easily. You may find it extremely hard to summon up those positive and encouraging feelings for yourself and this is entirely natural. As with many things you've read in this book, these things will not happen over night. They take time, determination, and dedication.

Try to give yourself recognition for anything you do that is praiseworthy. If you overcome a conflict with another person, no matter how difficult it was at the time, give yourself a pat on the back. If you face a fear, recognize it and feel good about yourself! Anytime you break out of your regular negative cycles and approach things from a different angle, take time to actively praise yourself and give yourself the kindness you deserve. Remember, your self-esteem belongs to you. Although having the approval of others can help keep us afloat, if we don't approve of ourselves we may as well sink. Seek to live a life that you can be proud of and enjoy every single step you take towards achieving your goals!

Self-Esteem and Getting What You Want From Life

In Part One, I touched lightly on the importance of setting realistic goals for yourself. Now that you are reaching the final stages of this part of your journey, I wanted to revisit this topic as it's one I believe should be at the front of our minds. Goal setting is an important part of everyone's life. It serves to motivate us, evaluate ourselves fairly, and shape our futures based on our own individual desires. Having something to look forward to is vital to your mood and overall outlook on life. Living a life which is monotonous or underwhelming can really put a dampener on your daily life not to mention having a negative effect on your self esteem. We need goals to mark our progression through life.

Setting and achieving goals can give your self-esteem and your self-confidence a real boost. It can really help to change the way you think about yourself and keep you feeling positive about the future. Thinking about what you want out of life and making plans to achieve those things is a great way to ensure personal growth and feel a sense of personal satisfaction. Each time we work hard to achieve a goal, we prove to ourselves that we are capable and deserving of more in life.

One of the most important parts of goal setting is being mindful of your capabilities. Often in life we set goals for ourselves that are almost impossible to achieve. We put unreasonable expectations on ourselves and end up feeling worse for it when we fail to live up to them. I can't stress enough the importance of making sure that the goals you set for yourself are *realistic*. The thing about goals is that they often require you to take multiple steps towards achieving them. For this reason, sometimes it's more beneficial to refrain from thinking about the end goal and place a few other goals you can hit along the way. For instance, let's say you decided that you wanted to run marathon but you've never done any running in your life. It's entirely possible that you will be able to run a marathon eventually but you'll have to do some training first.

Rather than setting the marathon as your goal, you'll be better off setting a few smaller goals that you can achieve along the way. Perhaps you start by setting a goal to run one mile, then three, then five. Each time you hit one of these smaller, more attainable goals, you're spurring yourself on, getting ever closer to running that marathon. With each goal you achieve, you feel more capable and confident. This is a very basic example but I'm sure you can see where I'm going with this. If we use goal setting to our advantage by keeping our goals realistic and achievable, we're more likely to reach them and continue moving forward in life. The more goals we achieve, the more likely we are to continue setting goals, thus encouraging ourselves towards living happier, more fulfilling lives.

A common pitfall when it comes to goal setting is trying to change too much too soon. If you find yourself in a slump and you're feeling like everything in your life needs an overhaul, you might fall into a habit like this. You're in a state of discontent so you decide that on Monday you're going to start dieting, quit smoking, write up a chore list to keep the house in better order, et cetera. These tendencies are dangerous as they're unrealistic and place you under an unreasonable amount of pressure. Life overhauls like this are almost impossible to achieve; therefore, they often mean setting yourself up for failure. Eventually you're likely to give up on the whole thing leaving yourself feeling under confident and dissatisfied.

Ask yourself now:
*Do you regularly set goals for yourself? If so, are they realistic?
*Do you reward yourself or give yourself credit when you achieve your goals?
*Do you often set yourself up for failure by trying to change too much too soon?
*Do you often give up on your goals?
*Do you rarely set goals at all? If so, how does that make you feel?

Without having realistic goals to work towards you might be starving yourself of things to feel good about. The act of goal setting itself succeeds in sending a positive message to yourself, one that says you believe in yourself and you want better for yourself. You're telling yourself that you can do this, you can have more, you are capable of living the life you want. And the closer to get to achieving your goals, the better you will feel about yourself. This is an active, practical way you can increase your feelings of self worth.

Exercise #9

Think about any goals you are currently working toward.

Ask yourself:

Are these goals realistic?
If not, how can I alter them in a way that will make them more attainable?
How will I feel if I achieve my goals?
How will I feel if I do not?
Is my life lacking in goals entirely?
Will I be able to survive if I fail?
Will I be able to celebrate if I achieve my goals?

Now take about a half an hour to formulate some realistic goals or alter any unrealistic goals you've already set for yourself. Get a piece of paper and write down some things you would like to achieve in the next 3 to 6 months. Think about all areas of your life and really focus on things that matter to you. Think about your career, your family life, your love life, your physical and mental well-being.

Refrain from writing down vague ideas like *"I want to be happy"*. Instead, write down some specific things that could bring you happiness. Remember that these goals should be things you can achieve in the next 3 to 6 months, not things that could take years to achieve!

Be careful not to overstretch yourself. For instance, try to steer clear of writing down things like, *"I want to lose 30lbs"*. Instead, if you'd like to work on your body, keep it positive by focusing your goal on looking and feeling better. This is important in order to prevent you from becoming low or beating yourself up if you don't achieve that goal.

When you've finished your list of goals, get another piece of paper and write down things you can DO to actively reach your goals. Think about the steps you will have to take between now and then. For instance, if you wrote that you would like to feel a greater sense of peace and serenity, write down some ways in which you can achieve those things such as practicing yoga, meditation, or spending more time doing the things you love. If you wrote that you would like to be in better physical health, you might think about cutting out some bad habits and getting more exercise. Try to be as specific as possible with these steps in order to keep your mind actively engaged with the goal setting process.

Once you've got your two lists to hand, place them somewhere where you will see them every day. Stick them on your refrigerator or your bathroom mirror. Take time every day to look at your lists. When you've taken steps towards reaching your goals, put a star or check beside them. If you think of other ways you can achieve your goals, add them to your list of steps. Try to actively engage with your goals on a daily basis and give yourself a pat on the back every time you do something that will help you achieve them.

When your 3 to 6 months are up, reflect on how this process worked for you. Write lists for the next 3 to 6 months using the skills and knowledge you gained from it. If you feel as though altering this exercise might benefit you, feel free to do so. Just remember to keep your goals realistic and achievable.

Living For Today With Confidence

As you have progressed through this book I've encouraged you to think back over your life and identify how your relationships and experiences helped to shape who you are. But I have also stressed a number of times how important it is to refrain from *reliving* your past. The past can be a great reference point when we are seeking to get to know ourselves better; however, it does not define you. As human beings, one of our greatest strengths is that we do not have to be stagnant beings. We have the ability to grow and change throughout our lives. We can make our lives what we want them to be. If there are things we don't like about ourselves, we can change them. We can learn from the past, recognize where things went wrong and seek to understand how certain events contributed to our self-beliefs. We do not, however, need to cling to the past.

Understanding more about ourselves and how we got where we are is extremely valuable, but the past is not something we can change. Spending too much time thinking about the past can rob you of the energy you need for life in the present. The real power we possess as human beings is the ability to make our lives what we want them to be in the here and now. Really try to tap into the power and use it to your benefit.

For those of us who had difficult childhoods or have experienced traumatic events throughout our lives, it can be hard to let go of anxiety about what lies in the future as well as letting go of regret about things that happened in the past. It can be hard to get perspective on the more challenging parts of life. Difficult situations can feel monumental, negativity can be all consuming. But it is up to us as individuals to make things easier on ourselves. The world can be hard enough on us! What we need is to stop being our own worst enemies and start to become our own best friends.

If you find yourself feeling weighed down by the past, encourage yourself to set yourself free from it. Give yourself permission to cut it loose. Focus on *today*. This is a time in your life where you can allow yourself to be light. Life needn't be all heartache and strife.

Make a vow to yourself to *enjoy* life. There will always be difficult times ahead but worrying about them will not change that. Taking care of yourself today will better equip you for any hurdles you might face in the future.

For people who have struggled with low self-esteem, letting go of the past can be an especially powerful accomplishment. It means forgiving yourself for any shortcomings and resisting the temptation to wallow in past mistakes. It means accepting yourself for who you are and forgetting about any ill feelings you once had for yourself. Letting go of the past means saying goodbye to any pain that has been inflicted on you by others letting yourself heal from heartaches that have held you down throughout your life. By freeing yourself from the grips of past regrets and future worries, you will be fully able to life for today.

Exercise #10

Take 15 to 20 minutes to think about yourself in light of everything you've learned from this book.

Ask yourself:

What have I learned about myself?
Has anything in my life or my self-beliefs already benefited from my dedication to feel better about myself?
How do I feel now compared to how I felt at the beginning of this journey?
Am I learning to value myself more?
Are my relationships starting to benefit from my self-growth?
Has it become easier for me to practice regular self-care?
How can I continue to grow and feel better about myself from now on?

Think about how much work you've put in and give yourself credit for it!

Get a piece of paper and write at least five things you like about yourself today. This may seem silly but it can be a powerful exercise. Resist the urge to do this in your head. Make sure you physically write these things down. When you have done so, reflect. Would you have been able to do that exercise at the beginning of your journey? Do you think that in the future you might be able to write 10 or 15 things on that list?

As one final exercise, I encourage you to think about your future and what you'd like your life to be like as time goes on. Make a vow to yourself to make your life what you want to be. Make a vow to be good to yourself, to treat yourself well, and to value your opinions and your feelings. Promise yourself that you'll be good yourself and feel proud of all your achievements as you progress through life.

Your Self-Esteem, Your Life. Live it.

"Happiness is not something you postpone for the future; it is something you design for the present."
Jim Rohn

When you finish reading this book, your journey of self-discovery will not end. You will have the rest of your life to continue growing and learning. The world is yours for the taking! Remember that no matter how much time and energy you put towards ultimate happiness, there will always be times in life when things are unpleasant or difficult. That is simply the nature of life. But I hope that you feel like you are now better equipped when it comes to overcoming these challenges. I hope that you will continue treating yourself well. No matter what the future brings you, I hope that you will continue on your journey towards truly loving yourself.

Allow yourself to have all the best things in life. Never stop respecting and valuing yourself. You have the power to take all the new skills you've developed here - all the ideas and understanding you now have - and stretch them even further, making your life what you want it to be. I wish you all the very best.

Your life belongs to you now. What will you do with it?

68426707R00071

Made in the USA
San Bernardino, CA
02 February 2018